DIY House Hacks: Clever Fixes for Modern Living

DIY House Hacks, Volume 1

RC PRABIR

Published by RC PRABIR, 2024.

DIY HOUSE HACKS: CLEVER FIXES FOR MODERN LIVING

First edition. November 19, 2024.

Copyright © 2024 RC PRABIR.

ISBN: 979-8230972020

Written by RC PRABIR.

Also by RC PRABIR

DIY House Hacks
DIY House Hacks: Clever Fixes for Modern Living

Table of Contents

DIY House Hacks:

Clever Fixes for Modern Living
By
RC Prabir

Preface

Welcome to -DIY House Hacks: Clever Fixes for Modern Living. This book is more than just a guide—it's your partner in tackling home repairs and maintenance with confidence and creativity.

Every home tells a story, and along with its charm come the inevitable challenges: a squeaky bed, a dripping tap, or a tricky paint job. These moments can feel overwhelming, but they're also opportunities to learn, innovate, and make your living space uniquely yours.

This book is designed for homeowners, renters, and DIY enthusiasts alike—anyone who wants practical solutions to everyday problems without calling in a professional. Whether you're solving a nagging issue or embarking on a creative project, you'll find easy-to-follow tips, clear instructions, and helpful insights to guide you.

In these pages, we focus on approachable, time-saving techniques. You don't need to be a seasoned handyman or have an arsenal of tools to succeed. Instead, you'll discover that with a bit of ingenuity and the right guidance, you can fix, revamp, and modernize your space in ways you never thought possible.

I hope this book inspires you to roll up your sleeves and embrace the joy of making things work better—because a little effort today can transform your home into a more comfortable, functional, and stylish haven tomorrow.

Let's get started and see just how rewarding DIY can be!

— Author and Publisher

Disclaimer

The information provided in **DIY House Hacks: Clever Fixes for Modern Living** is for general informational and educational purposes only. While every effort has been made to ensure the accuracy and reliability of the content, the author and publisher assume no responsibility for errors, omissions, or damages resulting from the use of this book. Readers are encouraged to use their discretion and seek professional advice when needed.

The techniques and suggestions in this book are based on the author's personal experiences and research. Results may vary depending on factors such as materials used, individual skill levels, and the condition of your home. Always follow safety protocols, use appropriate tools, and consult with a licensed professional for repairs or installations requiring specialized expertise.

Product names, trademarks, or brands mentioned in this book are the property of their respective owners. Any reference to specific products or services is for illustrative purposes only and does not constitute endorsement or recommendation by the author or publisher.

This book is protected under copyright law. No part of this publication may be reproduced, distributed, or transmitted in any form or by any means without the prior written permission of the author or publisher, except for brief quotations used in reviews or educational contexts.

By using the information in this book, readers agree to assume full responsibility for their actions and decisions. The author and publisher disclaim all liability for any loss or injury resulting from the use of materials or methods presented herein.

Thank you for respecting the intellectual property rights of this book and practicing responsible DIY!

How to fix a leaking toilet?

The flush toilet is an everyday object that we often pay little attention to. However, understanding how it works could save us some inconvenience. What are the causes of water leaks?

- **How does a toilet flush work?**
- **Possible causes of a leaking toilet flush**
- **How to avoid this problem?**

If you have a leaking toilet , don't delay in fixing it. This problem can cause significant waste: up to 600 liters of water per day. But before calling a plumber, make sure that the water leak cannot be repaired by yourself. Zoom in on how a toilet flush works and the possible causes of this flow.

How does a toilet flush work?

The mechanism of a flush toilet includes:

- a push button;
    - a float;
    - a water tap;
    - a drain valve.

When you press the flush button, several mechanisms take place.

1. The drain valve opens. The water accumulated in the tank quickly flows into the toilet . The waste and water present in the bowl are thus evacuated towards the sewerage pipes .

2. Once the tank is emptied, the valve closes to stop the flow. The float , an accessory for regulating the water level, detects the absence of water in the tank.

3. The water tap then opens to refill the tank. Once the water level is restored, the float rises, which triggers the tap to close.

Possible causes of a leaking toilet flush

Float adjustment and condition

Improper adjustment or deterioration of the float and its mechanism can cause a flush leak. In fact, a water level that is too high in the tank may cause the bowl to overflow during the next flush. Conversely, a level that is too low can cause the faucet to flow continuously, since the float does not rise enough to close it.

Water tightness of the water inlet and tank joints

If the water inlet seal is leaking due to wear or scale , this can cause water to leak outside the tank. The seal between the bowl and the tank can also deteriorate and cause a leak at this location.

A valve malfunction

A valve that does not close properly causes a constant flow of water into the bowl. It is possible that this problem is linked to scaling of this element. In this case, you can pour a little white vinegar into the tank.

The state of the tank

Finally, it may be that your tank is cracked or damaged. Unfortunately, there is no other solution than to replace it.

How to avoid this problem?

A leaking toilet is not without consequences. In addition to its impact on the cost of your water bills, it causes a significant waste of water , which is also detrimental to the environment.

With regular maintenance , you will extend the life of your flush.

• Check the condition of internal parts regularly. Replace them when they are defective.

• Clean these parts every six months to a year to remove dirt and lime scale that has accumulated in the tank. The frequency depends mainly on the water quality in your area.

• Check the float setting regularly and adjust it if necessary.

Water meter: how to check that there are no leaks?

Essential for properly monitoring your water consumption, the meter can sometimes be used to detect a water leak. How to read it? How to take a reading? All our answers.

SUMMARY

- **How do I read my water meter?**
- **How do I read my water meter?**
- **How to detect a leak by looking at the meter?**

Essential for accurately determining a household's consumption, reading the water meter is an important operation for establishing your bill or detecting potential water leaks . How to read your meter correctly? How to read it accurately? Find out how to determine your actual water consumption .

How do I read my water meter?

It is recommended that you have your water meter read every six months for the purpose of issuing your bill, and as frequently as necessary to ensure that the meter is working properly.

Sub-meters, commonly called water meters, measure the amount of water consumed in a plumbing installation in private homes. There are two types:

1. Volume meters, with two dials: a black one indicating consumption in cubic meters, and a red or white dial.
2. Speedometers, with a single dial that shows white numbers on a black background.

To read your water meter, carefully lift the cover. You will see a series of numbers:

- The **numbers on a black background** represent the meter reading in cubic meters (m^3) equivalent to 1000 liters, the only unit taken into account for billing.
- The **numbers on a red background** , although not included in the invoice, indicate units less than a cubic meter (hectoliters, deciliters, liters, and sometimes deciliters) and can help detect a leak.

Please note that you can install a connected smart meter that transmits your water consumption in real time to your water supplier for precise monitoring and not according to the estimated quantity of water volume.

Regardless of the type of meter, the index displayed corresponds to the quantity of water consumed since the meter was put into service or reset. To find out the water consumption over the past period, subtract the quantity previously recorded from the quantity currently displayed.

And to calculate the amount of your bill, multiply the quantity in m³ by the unit price mentioned on your subscription contract.

How do I read my water meter?

The annual water meter reading is generally carried out by a technician from the Water and Sanitation Union or by a person appointed by the community. During this operation, the technician can report any anomalies, including water leaks, and provide advice.

If you are not present when he comes, the technician will leave a pre-paid card in your mailbox , to be returned completed.

Once you have located the meter, you need to read your meter:

- Locate the decimal point, with whole numbers being one color, often black on a white background, and fractions on the other side of the decimal point in red.
- The unit to note is the cubic meter, excluding liters, hectoliters, deciliters, etc.
- The value taken must be noted on a piece of paper, indicating the unit.

Then send these numbers to the water supply company, either via the pre-paid card, by telephone or online from your customer area.

This survey is essential for quantifying actual consumption and establishing the annual bill, thus contributing to efficient management of water resources.

How to detect a leak by looking at the meter?

If you find your bill too high or have the impression that there is a water leak in your home, you can confirm this by observing your meter.

To confirm the presence of a leak, follow these steps:

- Record the consumption in deciliters;
- Close all faucets and the toilet valve ;
- Wait a few minutes;
- Read the deciliter figure again;
- If the latter has changed, this indicates a leak in the internal piping network .

In fact, in the event of a major leak, the deciliter figures will increase even when all the taps are closed. You will then have to close the tap of each water supply, one after the other, until the water meter stops to identify where the leak is coming from. Another point to check: the rotating star in the center of the clock is an accurate indicator of water circulation. If it turns without use, a leak is likely. Quick leak detection is essential to avoid damage to your property and reduce your water bill.

Namely

In the event of abnormal overconsumption, the law requires the water supplier to notify the subscriber so that checks can be carried out and leaks repaired. In the absence of a warning or if the repairs are carried out within the following month, the customer will not pay the part of the bill exceeding double the average consumption.

Knowing how to read your meter correctly allows you to take a correct reading and ensure the accuracy of the amount of the water utility bill. Above all, it allows you to detect potential anomalies before it is too late.

How to hang wallpaper on walls?

Whether you're looking to hide an imperfect wall, add color to a room, or give character to your decor, wallpaper is an original solution. Discover what wallpaper really is, its advantages and disadvantages, and the key steps to successfully install it in your home.

SUMMARY

- **What is a tapestry?**
- **What are the advantages and disadvantages of a tapestry?**
- **How to hang wallpaper?**

Wall tapestry , long considered an outdated decorative element, is now back in the spotlight. Designers and decorators are boldly reinterpreting it, integrating it into contemporary interiors to create surprising atmospheres.

What is a tapestry?

The art of tapestry dates back to antiquity, where it was practiced by various civilizations such as ancient Greece, Egypt and imperial China. It experienced a considerable boom in Europe from the 14th century onwards, with masterpieces such as The Lady and the Unicorn or The Hunts of Maximilian.

Over time, tapestry has also been modernized: artists such as Joan Miró and Pablo Picasso have left their mark on this art with contemporary and abstract works, often made using the Jacquard stitch technique.

Unlike wallpaper , tapestry is a decorative textile work made by hand or on a loom. This weaving generally represents ornamental, historical or mythological scenes. The term "tapestry" includes several meanings:

1. **Needlepoint** : Also called "petit poin", this technique consists of embroidering a pattern on a canvas, using counted stitches. It is frequently used for small decorative pieces such as cushions or wall panels.
2. **Hand-woven tapestry** : This traditional form is made on a high-warp (vertical warp threads) or low-warp (horizontal threads) loom. The weaver uses colored weft threads to create intricate patterns, completely covering the warp threads. These tapestries, often large in size, were designed to decorate the walls of castles , churches or noble residences.
3. **Wall hanging** : more generally, tapestry refers to any decorative fabric stretched over a wall, regardless of the technique used (weaving, embroidery , etc.).
4. **Fabric panel** : Tapestry can also be presented in the form of large panels of worked fabric, applied along the walls.
5. **Wallpaper** : it also happens that the amalgamation is made between wallpaper and tapestry.

Traditionally, tapestry is made from wool, a material favored for its ability to retain heat well and to dye easily . Some pieces also incorporate silk, which gives a luminous appearance, or even gold and silver threads for the most prestigious works. Today, tapestry continues to find its place in modern interiors, combining tradition and modernity. It embodies an art in its own right, which adapts to contemporary decorative trends while perpetuating ancestral know-how.

What are the advantages and disadvantages of a tapestry?

Wall tapestries, often used to add a touch of elegance and originality to an interior, differ from wallpaper in their artisanal character and artistic dimension. Here are the advantages and disadvantages to consider when choosing a wall tapestry.

The advantages of a wall tapestry

A wall tapestry can be a work of art in its own right. Ornamental patterns, whether classic, abstract or inspired by nature, bring character, authenticity and unparalleled charm to a room.

Thanks to the thickness of its materials, the tapestry also improves the thermal and acoustic comfort of a room. It helps to reduce noise and maintain heat, which makes it particularly suitable for old or poorly insulated houses .

Tapestries offer a unique personalization: they can be custom-made to match the exact tastes and needs of a space. Plus, made of wool or silk, they are sturdy and can last for decades if properly maintained.

The Disadvantages of a Wall Tapestry

One of the main challenges with tapestries is their maintenance . The fabric, often fragile, can accumulate dust , and requires regular cleaning to prevent it from fading. Unlike a painted wall or wallpaper, they require specific care.

A quality tapestry, especially if it is handmade or custom-made, represents a significant investment. Its installation can be complex, especially if it is heavy, and often requires the intervention of professionals to ensure a secure attachment.

Although tapestry is versatile, it doesn't fit into every interior style. Some modern or sleek decors might be out of place with its sometimes busy or traditional look.

How to hang wallpaper?

Hanging a wall tapestry requires rigor and careful preparation. Unlike wallpaper, tapestry is a thick and heavy fabric, which makes its installation more technical. Here are the steps to follow for a successful and durable installation.

Preparing the wall

First of all, the wall must be carefully prepared. Make sure it is clean and free of dust . If there are any cracks or holes , fill them in to prevent these irregularities from damaging the wallpaper over time. If your wall is rough, a light sanding will allow you to obtain a smooth surface. Finally, make sure the wall is perfectly dry: humidity could cause mold ,[1] compromising both the fixing and the integrity of the fabric.

---

1. http://www.lefigaro.fr/maison/comment-nettoyer-de-la-moisissure-sur-des-murs-20221009

Choice of fixing system

The choice of fixing system depends on the size and weight of the tapestry, as well as the desired aesthetic effect.

A hanging bar (the most common):

A rod is attached to the wall , and the tapestry is hung using rings or hooks sewn onto the fabric. This system makes it easy to remove the tapestry for maintenance.

Velcro or hook and loop strips:

For lightweight tapestries, Velcro strips are a discreet solution that does not damage the fabric. They also allow the tapestry to be easily dismantled and reassembled.

A wooden frame:

As with a painting , the tapestry is stretched over a wooden frame , which gives it a rigid finish. This method is particularly suitable for a neat and formal presentation.

Invisible nails or hooks:

For a more traditional look, you can nail the tapestry directly to the wall using small nails or invisible hooks. However, this method can damage the fabric if done incorrectly.

Installing the wallpaper

Before hanging the tapestry, temporarily hang it to adjust its placement. Use a level to check that it is straight and centered on the wall.

Once the positioning is validated, fix the tapestry according to the chosen system. If you opt for a hanging bar, make sure that it is well fixed with screws adapted to the weight of the work.

For a flawless finish, adjust the tension of the tapestry by stretching it slightly to avoid creases. This ensures a smooth and even surface.

Please note:

Tapestries, especially those made of natural fibers, can fade if exposed to prolonged direct light. Consider installing curtains or blinds to filter the light and preserve the colors.

Hanging a wall tapestry requires a minimum of preparation and attention, but the result is worth it to bring an artistic and warm touch to your interior.

How to store opened paint pots?

To prevent the paint from deteriorating, it is important to close the can tightly.

When you carry out painting work, it is common to have leftover cans. Discover practical tips to extend the life of your paint and preserve its quality over time.

SUMMARY

- **Why is it important to store your paint pots properly?**
- **Where to store your leftover paint?**
- **How to store an opened pot of paint in good condition?**

Rather than throwing away your opened paint pots , why not save them for future touch-ups or projects? Here are our tips for storing and preserving them properly.

Why is it important to store your paint pots properly?

Keeping leftover paint after renovation work is both an economical and ecological approach. Indeed, keeping it allows you to touch up your walls or furniture , or even start future projects without having to buy new pots. This not only avoids waste, but also helps reduce waste production and overconsumption of resources.

To ensure that the paint retains its properties over time, it is important to store it properly. A poorly closed or poorly stored pot can cause the paint to dry quickly or deteriorate, rendering it useless.

Where to store your leftover paint?

To ensure that your leftover paint is properly preserved, you must take a few precautions. First of all, before storing your paint pot, whether it is glycerophthalic paint , acrylic paint or water-based paint, remember to note the date of purchase and the color on the container. This information can quickly be forgotten, especially if several years go by before you use the paint again.

Choosing a storage location is important. Choose a dry place, away from light and extreme temperatures. Significant variations in heat or cold will affect the quality of the paint. Excessive heat can cause solvents to evaporate, while extreme cold can cause paint to freeze, especially if it is water-based or latex. Therefore, avoid uninsulated garages or garden sheds exposed to the elements. A shelf inside the house, or in a well-insulated garage at room temperature, is ideal.

Finally, paint and humidity do not mix well. A humid environment can cause corrosion of the container, which would irreparably damage the paint. So, make sure to choose a dry place for long-lasting and optimal storage.

How to store an opened pot of paint in good condition?

Here are some practical tips to ensure optimal conservation:

1. **Avoid contact of paint with air:** as soon as you open a can of paint, air enters it, which causes oxidation by oxygen, creating a pasty film on the surface of the paint. To avoid this, limit exposure to air as much as possible by sealing the can tightly after each use.

2. **Keep the paint in its original container** : even if there is only a small amount of paint left in the pot, it is not recommended to transfer it to another container. The original pots are designed to ensure better conservation, in particular thanks to their opacity and airtightness. An unsuitable pot such as a transparent glass pot could let light through and alter the quality of the paint. However, if your pot is damaged, you can use a fluorinated bottle. This container is specially designed for paints containing solvents: it closes with a screw cap, and is perfectly airtight.

3. **Thoroughly clean the edges of the jar and lid** to remove any residue that could compromise the seal . You can place plastic wrap directly on the paint before closing the jar for optimal sealing.

4. **To properly close the jar,** use a rubber mallet to tap lightly along the edges of the lid to avoid damaging it and ensure a tight seal. You can reinforce this seal by wrapping adhesive tape around the lid, thus preventing any air infiltration.

5. **Store the jar** in a room at room temperature and stable

6. **Turn the closed paint can upside** down to prevent air from

coming into contact with the paint. Also, if a layer of paint were to dry, it would form at the bottom of the can, leaving the top part usable.

7. **Never mix multiple paints:** Each paint has a unique chemical composition, and mixing them could alter their properties, affecting texture, color or drying.

8. **Check the expiration date**
Paint cans usually have an expiration date on the label. Although this date is only indicative, it gives an idea of how long the paint can be used under optimal conditions. Properly stored paint can often last several years beyond this date.

By following these tips, you can extend the life of your paint cans and maintain their quality for future uses.

Putty, wood paste, glue... how to properly store your opened DIY products?

When doing DIY work, it is common to not use up all of products such as putty, wood filler or glue. What should you do with these products once they have been used? How can you store them? Our answers.

SUMMARY

- Why is it important to store your DIY products properly?
- Where to store leftover product?
- How to store them properly?

Opened pots and tubes of wood putty, putty or glue often end up stored in a corner, without you really knowing how to preserve them for later use. These leftovers can be valuable for future projects, provided you know how to store them properly. Find out why it is essential to store your opened DIY products properly, where to store [1] them to prevent them from deteriorating and, above all, how to preserve them in the best possible conditions.

Why is it important to store your DIY products properly?

Storing your DIY products properly is important for several reasons.

First, proper storage **extends the life of the products** . Whether it's glue or putty, these materials deteriorate quickly when not stored properly. Exposing them to air, humidity or temperature fluctuations can compromise their effectiveness, which will force you to throw them away and buy new ones. By storing your products carefully, **you avoid this unnecessary waste** .

Second, it's a question of economy. By extending the life of your DIY products and tools, you reduce your expenses in the long run. Well-preserved materials can be reused for future projects, allowing you to make your initial investments profitable.

Finally, there is an environmental issue that should not be overlooked. Throwing away partially used products or damaged tools contributes to the increase in waste . By taking care of your materials, **you limit the production of waste** and participate in a more environmentally friendly approach. Storing your DIY products optimally is therefore doing something for both your wallet and the planet.

Where to store leftover product?

Like food, some DIY products are also perishable. Storing your products correctly is not limited to closing the jars or tubes after use.

---

1. https://www.lefigaro.fr/lifestyle/2017/01/27/30001-20170127ARTFIG00217-comment-ranger-sa-maison-une-fois-pour-toutes.php

Where you store them also plays a role in their longevity. Be careful to avoid glass jars, as they are translucent and can let light through, thus accelerating the degradation of the product. In addition, the packaging containers are not always perfectly airtight, which can cause them to dry out quickly.

Wood putties and fillers, on the other hand, require similar conditions, but with special attention to temperature .[2] A cool, dry place, between 5 °C and 25 °C, is recommended to preserve their effectiveness. Protect them from frost and direct sunlight, as these elements can alter their texture and make them unusable. Thus, a garden shed or cellar can be suitable, provided that these spaces are well ventilated and do not undergo sudden changes in temperature.

Good to know

Paint ,[3] for example, is particularly sensitive to storage conditions.

How to store them properly?

When you start using DIY products like putty, glue or wood filler ,[4] you need to be careful to store them properly to prevent them from drying out or deteriorating.

The putty:

- After use, seal the nozzle well to prevent moisture from entering. If you are using a cartridge, squeeze a little sealant out of the tip of the nozzle and let it dry: this protective layer

---

2.   http://www.lefigaro.fr/maison/quelle-est-la-temperature-ideale-dans-une-maison-en-hiver-20221127

3. http://www.lefigaro.fr/maison/quelles-peintures-choisir-pour-repeindre-son-interieur-20230115

4. http://www.lefigaro.fr/maison/pourquoi-opter-pour-une-maison-a-ossature-en-bois-20230901

will prevent the rest of the product from drying out.

- For even longer storage, place the mastic in an airtight glass jar and cover with linseed oil . You can also use water mixed with a few drops of glycerin to prevent drying out.

Wood pulp:

- To save the wood paste, flatten its surface with a sheet of cling film and press it onto the paste before sealing the jar tightly.
- Store it in a cool place, ideally a workshop, to ensure its longevity.

The glue:

- Always close the container tightly, even if you need to use it again quickly. Make sure the tip is clean and dry before replacing the cap.
- Store glue in a cool, dry place away from heat and moisture, such as in a tightly sealed plastic bag or airtight bucket. If possible, store it in the refrigerator to extend its shelf life.
- To prevent crusting, repot the glue in a smaller, more suitable container, especially if there is little product left. This minimizes exposure to air and preserves the quality of the glue for longer. Don't forget to label the products so you can find them easily.

By following these tips, you will maximize the lifespan of your DIY products and avoid waste (and unpleasant surprises) during your next projects

Why can washing machines cause electric shocks?

Have you had the unpleasant surprise of getting an electric shock when taking your laundry out of the machine? There are several reasons why this could happen. Find out the causes and solutions.

SUMMARY

- Poor grounding
- The resistance is defective
- One of the cables is damaged
- Who to contact in case of discharges?

Shock, electric shock, chestnut, tingling... These are the effects you feel every time you touch your washing machine ? Does the electric joust increase if your hands are wet? These electric shocks should not be taken lightly. Learn to diagnose the origin of these inconveniences and above all to remedy them as soon as possible.

Poor grounding

The first reason for an electric shock via your washing machine is to be found on the plug side. Your appliance must first be connected to a dedicated 20 A socket: do not use a power strip for this high energy consuming appliance , like the oven or the hob .

Then examine the **earth connection of the socket** : this is the 3rd pin above the two holes for phase and neutral. This device protects you from electrocution by flowing the current to earth. If it is deficient or even absent, it is up to your body to conduct the electric current. Earthing is inseparable from the differential circuit breaker, which cuts the current in the event of a leak.

Caution

For the installation of a grounding system, it is recommended to call a professional.

The resistance is defective

The heating element is the part that heats the water in the washing machine and then maintains its temperature. It is located near the tank and accessible from the front or side of the washing machine (refer to the instructions). If the connections are damaged, the heating element can trip your installation or cause electric shocks.

In concrete terms, the damaged resistor creates a "leakage current", meaning that the electricity passes through a path that was not initially intended. And often, it is through you that the current is routed. To locate this leak, use a multi meter.

- Turn off and unplug your washing machine
- Unscrew the rear panel or the resistance access hatch
- Remove the connectors (where the wires come from)

- Set the multimeter to the lowest Ohm value
- Place one of the probes on the connector and another on the chassis or the ground terminal: if the multimeter indicates a value, it means that there is current escaping from it.

One of the cables is damaged

Neither the resistance nor your grounding are responsible for the electric shocks? Then check the wiring of your washing machine. With the power off, open the socket to see if there are any melted or damaged cables.

Take the opportunity to check the differential circuit breaker (30 mA type A) on your electrical panel, which must play its role in the event of an electrical problem.

Who to contact in case of discharges?

Once the test is done, several options are available to you. If you are not comfortable with electricity, it is recommended to have a professional come by. To check the grounding, their use is also mandatory.

If you are familiar with electricity, changing cables will seem like an accessible and quick action.

Flashing light bulb: why and what to do?

Rarely dangerous, a light bulb that starts to flash is often annoying in a living room. Be aware that this phenomenon can have several causes depending on the type of bulb used. Discover the main explanations and solutions to remedy it effectively.

SUMMARY

- **What causes can explain a flashing light bulb?**
- **Can a flashing light bulb be dangerous?**
- **The light bulb is flashing: what to do?**

Whether it is a simple false contact, an incompatibility with the electrical circuit, or a more serious failure, it is better to quickly identify the source of a flashing bulb .

What causes can explain a flashing light bulb?

Regardless of the type of lamp used (table lamp , halogen lamp, bedside lamp, floor lamp , etc.), several causes can explain the flashing of a bulb:

- One of the common reasons is a **bad contact** due to the bulb not being properly fixed to the lamp or spotlight holder. Check if the bulb is correctly screwed into its socket, by switching off the power supply before any manipulation.
- Crackling or flashing when turning on or during use can also be the result of **a faulty component** in the bulb itself, particularly if the bulb is worn or too old.
- A **problem with the electrical installation**, incorrectly connected wiring to the light fixture or a faulty switch may be the cause.
- If **the switch is dirty**, a simple cleaning may be enough, but if it is old, it is better to replace it.
- A **transformer malfunction,** especially if connected to multiple bulbs, can cause variations in light intensity. Replacement of this component may then be necessary.
- **Overheating of light bulbs**, especially fluorescent and neon lights, which can flicker due to voltage variations.
- An **electrical system design problem**, such as poor circuit separation, can cause multiple bulbs to flash simultaneously, especially if there is an overcurrent or overconsumption from a device plugged into the same circuit. In this case, consult a professional electrician for an accurate diagnosis.

Can a flashing light bulb be dangerous?

Although a flickering light bulb is usually due to a benign electrical problem, it can sometimes pose dangers. Possible risks include:

- **Eye** fatigue
- Headaches [1]
- An **epileptogenic risk** for photosensitive people

---

1. https://sante.lefigaro.fr/sante/symptome/maux-tete/quelles-causes

- Fires [2]
- In very rare cases, **explosions** .

For example,

an incandescent light bulb, which produces light by heating a filament, can overheat and possibly catch fire if flammable materials are nearby. Although these bulbs are no longer commercially available, they still pose a danger in some older installations. The **risk of explosion is even rarer** , but possible for incandescent bulbs, fluorescent tubes or halogen lamps. This danger occurs in the event of excessive overheating, manufacturing defects or old equipment, which can weaken the structure of the bulb. On the other hand, energy-saving LED bulbs, which generate less heat, considerably reduce these risks.

While some problems can be easily solved, others require the intervention of a professional electrician. Our advice: invest in quality bulbs to avoid these inconveniences and ensure the safety of your installation.

Please note

You can install anti-flicker filters on energy-saving LED bulbs to avoid unpleasant effects.

The light bulb is flashing: what to do?

If your bulb flickers immediately after installation, check that it is the correct type of bulb and that it is screwed in correctly. If necessary, replace it with a new, better quality model that can better withstand voltage fluctuations.

If a bulb already in place is flickering, try to identify the origin of the problem to see if it comes from the bulb itself or from the electrical

---

2. http://www.lefigaro.fr/maison/maison-en-feu-que-faire-comment-reagir-20230121

circuit . To do this, start by installing another one that works correctly in place of the defective bulb.

- If the flashing continues, the bulb is probably the cause and needs to be replaced.
- If it lights up normally, the problem is rather in the electrical circuit.

It is also possible that the problem comes from

your switches or the dimmer, especially if the bulb used is not compatible with these devices. Some LED bulbs, for example, are not always compatible with dimmers, which can cause flickering. In this case, installing dimmers with interference filters, designed to eliminate residual currents, can be effective.

If, despite these checks, the flashing persists, it is recommended to have your electrical installation inspected by a professional. Bulbs are sensitive to voltage variations and repeated problems can indicate instability in the electrical network. An electrician will be able to detect possible current leaks or overconsumption and advise you on the measures to take, including contacting your electricity supplier to have the transformers checked. If in doubt, the intervention of a professional remains the best option to secure and bring your electrical installation up to standard.

Why don't I have any hot water pressure? What should I do?

Low hot water pressure can have several origins.

When you are going to take a shower, it's just a drip of water that runs from the showerhead. Same thing when you have to do your dishes. Let's examine the reasons for this fall in performance, and especially how to fix the whole problem easily.

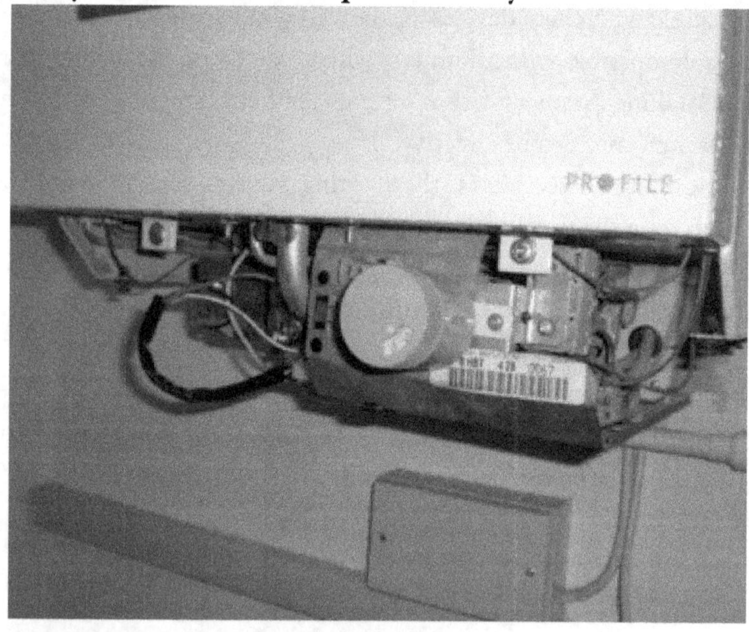

SUMMARY

- Why do I have low hot water flow?
- How to increase hot water pressure?

A low flow rate of hot water is a real handicap for everyday life. A number of causes can explain this drop in pressure. An overview of the possible causes and solutions to resolve the situation.

Why do I have low hot water flow?

If the loss of pressure concerns the cold and hot water in your home, first eliminate the hypothesis of a general problem: your town, neighborhood or residence may be impacted by a distribution or leak problem. Then contact the water department, to whom you pay the bill, or your condominium trustee .

If only your home is affected, look for a pipe leak . In addition to the cost incurred , a leak affects the distribution of water in your home and therefore its pressure. To prove it, turn off all the taps and check if your water meter is still running. Contact a plumber to fix it.

If there is no leak , check the water supply to your home (near your meter): a half-closed valve affects the water pressure. Open it completely.

Then take a look at your pressure reducer, a small element placed near your water heater or hot water tank, designed to limit the pressure in your pipes . If necessary, adjust it. Be careful, not all water heaters have a reducer.

Finally, white vinegar will be useful if only a mixer tap or a shower are struggling: scale is often responsible for this variation. unscrew and open the aerators of your taps and the water holes of your shower- head and clean them with some anti-scale white vinegar. If necessary, replace your defective taps.

How to increase hot water pressure?

You've tested all your faucets, and the problem only occurs when you use hot water? After that you need to turn on your water heater.

Start with a quick check of your installation :

presence or absence of corrosion, leak check, suspicious noises . The thermostat and the pressure valve must also be checked. Then, remember to descale your tank. Scaling due to water that is too hard can cause a drop in flow rate.

If your appliance is electric, turn off the electricity and water and empty your pipes before starting to descale . Be careful when draining, because the temperature of the outlet water is high. Remember to place a bucket to collect it. When the fittings have been dismantled and the tank is completely emptied, access the tank and clean it carefully. This should give your installation a new lease of life and solve your both water flow and water pressure problems. Be careful, if you are not familiar with DIY or if your tank is difficult to access, call a professional instead .

What do dishwasher error codes mean?

Dishwasher fault codes differ depending on the appliance manufacturer

Each brand of dishwasher uses its own codes to signal faults: find out what they are to diagnose and possibly repair your appliance.

Is your dishwasher showing signs of malfunction? Does it stop mid-cycle, flash strangely or display an incomprehensible error code? These situations can be stressful, but error codes are designed to help you quickly identify the nature of the problem.

Electrolux

To find out the fault codes, consult the control panel of your dishwasher. Depending on the model of your Electrolux appliance, the error code may start with i or E.

- **AL5, C1, F1** : problem related to water supply.
- **C3:** Fault related to the appliance motor. See the cycling pump side.
- **C8:** Problem with the dishwasher temperature probe. The probe is integrated into the heating element.
- **i10:** Water filling detection problem in your dishwasher. Check if your faucet is properly connected to the water hose.
- **i20:** Drain problem in your dishwasher. Check the accessories, the tank filters and if there is a grease plug in the drain pipes.
- **i30** : Leak detected on the base of your dishwasher. The appliance goes into permanent drain or goes into safety mode. The anti-flood device is activated. Inspect the tap and the attachment of the water inlet hose, the cleanliness of the filters and the cycling arms.
- **i40, i43 or i44** : Pressure sensor and water level control failure. Make sure the filters are clean. The pressure switch (part that calculates the air and water inside the tank to determine the amount of water to fill and drain the appliance) is not configured properly. Try restarting your appliance to help it.
- **i50, i51, i52, i54, i55, i56, i56, i58, i55, i5a, i5h, i5c or i5h:** Drain problem. You need to clean the filters and spray arms, then unplug the dishwasher from the outlet, wait 60 seconds and plug it back in.
- **i60:** water heating problem in your dishwasher. This may come from the resistance.
- **i70** : problem with the temperature probe of the household appliance
- **i80:** communication problem between the electronic modules of your dishwasher.

- **i90** : programming anomaly in your household appliance .

To clear the fault codes stored in the device's memory, press and hold the start/pause button. The device can then restart its cycle normally.

Samsung

If there is a problem with your device, you may see a code appear on the control display:

- **3C, 3E** : Pump malfunction. Turn off the dishwasher and restart it.
- **4C, 4E** : Water supply problem to your dishwasher. Check that the water supply valve is open or if the water supply is interrupted.
- **5C, 5E** : Drain problem. Close the water supply valve. Inspect the drain hose as it may be clogged or kinked.
- **9E** : Water level problem which may be caused by a faulty pressure switch.
- **4E1** : Temperature problem. It appears when the water is above 75°.
- **AC** : Communications failure between primary and secondary card.
- **BC2, BE2:** A button is stuck. Try to unlock it with your fingers. If your screen is touch-sensitive, remove any traces of moisture or foreign objects using a dry cloth.
- **HC, HE** : heating error, often caused by a faulty resistor.
- **HE1, TE1** : thermostat or temperature sensor malfunction .[1]
- **LC, LE** : A rinse arm is blocked.
- **OC** : means there is too much water.

---

1. http://www.lefigaro.fr/maison/comment-installer-un-thermostat-connecte-chez-soi-20221113

- **OE** : Overload in your dishwasher.
- **PC, PE:** water distribution failure. This frequently happens when an alternating valve is faulty.

Bosch

The fault information appears on the device's control panel. Either the fault code is displayed or you can observe the number of times the indicator lights flash.

- **E01** : problem related to the resistance or the electronic card of your device.
- **E02, E04** : heating element failure
- **E03** : Malfunction of the resistance working relay. The electronic card, the additional resistance working relay and the resistance must be checked.
- **E05** : Continuous water switching problem.
- **E06** : Hall Sensor is not functional.
- **E07** : Drying problem. Check that your dishwasher fan is working properly.
- **E08** : Problem with the heating element of the appliance.
- **E09** : A problem with the resistance or the electronic card of your dishwasher.
- **E10** : problem with heating devices with zeolite drying.
- **E11, E12, E13** : the appliance does not heat.
- **E14** : When starting a wash cycle, this error code indicates a problem filling the appliance. Check the water inlet tap, if the solenoid valve filter is not clogged or if the appliance's Aquastop is faulty.
- **E15:** A water leak has been detected within the appliance. The drain hose is dirty, kinked, cracked or the Aquastop leak protection system is activated.

- **E16 or E17** : failure to fill your dishwasher, generally caused by a fault in the filling valve.
- **E18** : Waiting for water to arrive. Inspect the Aquastop water supply hose of your dishwasher: it must be in perfect working order.
- **E19** : Indicates a fault in the heat exchanger valve or the valve located on the product box. They will need to be replaced.
- **E20** : Problem with the cycling pump of your dishwasher.
- **E21** : Pump blockage. Check that nothing is obstructing the pump. Change it if it is damaged.
- **E22** : Dishwasher filter fault. The drain pump reports difficulty in draining the wash water.
- **E23** : fault in the appliance drain pump. You notice the presence of water in the bottom of the dishwasher tub or abnormal noises emitted by the appliance.
- **E24** : Partial or total drain problem. The washing or rinsing water is no longer drained out of the appliance.
- **E25** : Complete absence of drainage. Check all elements concerned with the proper drainage of water (drain pump, drain pipe, non-return valve, heat exchanger).
- **E26** : Water supply fault.
- **E27** : Low DC voltage problem.
- **E28** : AquaSensor malfunction. Check that it is properly connected and clean.
- **E29** : Power supply fault of the appliance. Insufficient electrical voltage (voltage lower than 170-190 V) or overvoltage problem.
- **E30** : internal fault detection.
- **E31** : problem linked to the zeolite resistance of the device, which could come from a dirty water probe.
- **E3000 , E3100, E3200 , E3300** : water supply anomaly.

- **E3400** : Problem with the water supply or the AquaStop system.
- **E6101**, **E6102**, **E6103** : The water in your dishwasher cannot drain properly. Your dishwasher is not draining properly.
- **E6104** : Problem with the resistor or the electronic card.
- **E6900** : Malfunction of the heat exchanger or the product box.
- **E9240** : water evacuation anomaly.

Brandt

These fault codes are indicated either by flashing lights or by a direct display of the error code on the dashboard.

- **01** : Filling problem. Check the water inlet, the solenoid valve and the water level sensor.
- **02** : Drainage problem which may come from the drain pump, the drain pipes or the water level detector.
- **03** : Heating problem, caused either by a resistance or probe fault. It can also be a door safety problem.
- **04** : probe problem.
- **05** : Pump problem.
- **06** : blocked drain pump problem which could come from the pump turbine or a blockage.
- **07** : Leakage problem.
- **08** : Problem with reversing the washing arms. The arm alternation system may indeed be defective. Check their positioning.
- **011** : Failure at the pressure sensor level on the cycling pump.
- **012** : Filling fault. Check the evacuation system.
- **013** : temperature problem which may be caused by the

heating relay, the sensor or the card.

- **014** : Incorrect water level in the dishwasher or the pump is defective.
- **Ed** : corresponds to a communication error between the electronic boards. Reset the device by unplugging it for 10 min.
- **Rapid** **light** flashes: longer water supply delay. The tap is closed, the water supply is blocked or the water pressure is too low.
- The *Glass* light flashes quickly: overflow. A component of the dishwasher is leaking.

De Dietrich

The fault code is displayed on the control panel of your De Dietrich dishwasher as soon as the fault occurs.

- **E01** : Dishwasher filling problem. Check the tap, water inlet hose and solenoid valve.
- **E02** : Drainage problem in the dishwasher to be found on the drain pump and drain pipe side. At the same time, check that the level detection system is working properly
- **E03** : Heating problem. Check the heating element and the probe. The door safety may be the cause of the fault.
- **E4** : Failure of the temperature probe in the dishwasher.
- **E5** : Pump problem in the dishwasher. It may be cut off or disconnected. Check the condition of the part and change it if necessary.
- **E6** : Blocked pump problem in the dishwasher. Make sure the pump impeller is working properly during its start-up phase.
- **E7** : Water leak or overflow problem . Review the filler pipe, gaskets ,[2] filler hose.

- **E8** : Pressure sensor problem on the cycling pump of your dishwasher. Check that the motor that allows the waste water to be evacuated is not disconnected and that the propeller is not blocked.
- **E12** : The dishwasher empties and fills at the same time. The cause of the malfunction is to be found in the drain system, the water tap, the solenoid valve or the filling system.
- **E13** : Temperature problem. The heating circuit is affected. Check the electronic card and the resistor.
- **E14** : Water level problem. Check the water flow, the filter on the faucet, the water supply circuit. The pump may also be out of order.

Jump

Here are the fault codes for the Sauter brand:

- **D01** : Water supply fault. Check the tap.
- **D02** : Dishwasher drain problem.
- **D03** : Device heating fault.
- **D04** : Temperature sensor fault.
- **D05** : Pump current fault too low.
- **D06** : Pump current fault too high.
- **D07** : Overflow/Anti-leak malfunction.
- **D08** : watering distribution problem.
- **D11** : Pressure sensor fault.
- **D12** : Water level fault. Siphon with the drain hose.
- **D13** : Overheating problem.
- **D14** : Drain pipe connection incorrectly made, or tap flow too low or filters clogged
- **The lights all come on one after the other** : incorrect

---

2. http://www.lefigaro.fr/maison/comment-retirer-et-refaire-un-joint-en-silicone-20240710

programming. Cancel the current programming by pressing the start button for three seconds, then start programming again.

- **A light flashes**, **the program does not start** : depending on the model, this may be due to the wrong position of the program selector (between two notches). Position the selector correctly opposite the program.

Whirlpool

Is your Whirlpool dishwasher showing you an error code or flashing? Here's what it means.

- **F1** : The temperature probe is faulty and prevents the machine from starting or has an impact on the quality of the selected washing mode.
- **F2** : Water leak signal. Drain the lost liquid by removing the plate at the back of your device.
- **F3** : breakdown or fault in the heating circuit, due to a malfunction in the wiring or the resistance.
- **F4** : Drainage problem, which may come from the filters or the drain pipe.
- **F5** : Circulation pump malfunction. Replace if necessary.
- **F6** : No water supply. Turn on the water supply or examine the hose, which may be kinked.
- **F7** : Poor water supply. Check that the water flow and the tap are properly open.
- **F8** : Failure related to the water level in the tank. Clean the filters and the bottom of the tank. Then press the Start button for five seconds.
- **F9** : Too much water in your Whirlpool dishwasher. The problem may come from the solenoid valve, the pressure

switch, the compression chamber or the electronic card.

- **F10** : Dirt detection probe problem.
- **F11 or FA** : Water inlet presence detector malfunction. If the FA fault code is displayed, quickly change the water inlet hose.
- **F12 or FB** : Malfunction of the motor that redirects water to the wash arms.
- **F13** : Wash arm malfunction. Water is no longer distributed.
- **F14** : Memory saturation of your Whirlpool dishwasher.
- **F15** : malfunction of your electronic card memory.

Candy

If your machine does not have a display, count the number of flashes of the flashing light to find out the fault number.

- **E02, E2** : Water filling problem. Make sure the water supply system tap is open, the pipes are not clogged or in poor condition.
- **E03, E3** : Drainage problem which may be caused by the pump and the drain pipe.
- **E04, E4** : detection of a water leak.
- **E05, E5** : Problem with the water temperature reading system. Check the status of the temperature probe.
- **E06, E6** : Electronic card configuration problem.
- **E07, E7** : problem with the motor, the circulation pump or the washing pump.
- **E08, E8** : water heating problem which may come from the heating resistor, the water detection system or the circulation pump.
- **E09, E9** : fault in the dirt detection probe.
- **E10, Ea** : program selector reading fault.

- **E12, Ec** : Motor, cycling pump or wash pump rotation malfunction.
- **E14, Ee** : heating circuit problem which could come from the resistor, the pressure detector or the electronic card.
- **E15, Ef** : Too much water in the appliance. Filling is too fast.
- **E16, Eh** : Problem with the pressure sensor.
- **E17, Ei:** heating power supply malfunction. You can replace the electronic card of your dishwasher.
- **E18, El** : problem with water control which may come from the solenoid valve or the pressure switch.
- **E21, E22, E23, and E24** : problem draining the appliance, probably due to a blockage.
- **ES** : water supply problem
- **SL** : The salt pot is empty.

LG

The fault code of your LG dishwasher can be read directly on the front panel of the appliance.

- **AE or E1** : Possible leak from the appliance. This error code also indicates the possibility of a spill or that the appliance is not properly leveled.
- **BE** : use of inappropriate detergent .
- **CE, LE** : Problem with the motor or the electrical harness between the motor and the control panel of your dishwasher.
- **CD** : This code indicates the start of an additional drying cycle.
- **CL** : dishwasher child safety device activated.
- **CR** : The device is in test mode. To disable it, turn off the device. Wait two minutes and then turn it back on.
- **EI:** The drain pump has started to operate automatically,

which means that there is probably a water leak at the pipe connections. Turn off the water supply and unplug your dishwasher.

- **F** : The machine assesses the clarity of the water.
- **FE:** abnormal increase in the quantity of water in your household appliance. The problem certainly comes from the solenoid valve which allows the circulation of water to be authorized or interrupted.
- **HE** : LG dishwasher heating circuit fault. This can come from different parts such as the resistor, the wires or the resistor terminals which have poor contact.
- **IE:** Water is not coming into the appliance. Check the water pressure and the drain hose outlet installation.
- **NE:** error in the cario motor which controls the dishwasher spray arms.
- **OE** : Water is not being pumped or drained into your dishwasher. Clean the filter, check for food debris and the pump is in good condition.
- **PF** : A power outage has occurred.
- **TE** : Heating problem. The device has experienced a thermal error.

Please note

The device may also display **2H** . This is not an error code, but an estimate of the time remaining for the cycle to complete. That is 2 hours.

Siemens

Depending on the model of your Siemens dishwasher, you can read this code on an electronic display or by observing the number of flashes of the indicator lights.

- **CD** : start an additional drying cycle.
- **CL** : dishwasher child safety device activated.
- **E01** : Electronic problem. The dishwasher must be turned off and then restarted.
- **E09** : heating problem. Check the resistance or the cycling pump.
- **E15** : There is water in the floor tank. Check where the leak is coming from and change the seals if necessary.
- **E22** : The appliance filter needs to be cleaned.
- **E24** : Check the drainage system
- **EI** : Water leak at the pipe connections. Turn off the water supply and unplug your dishwasher.
- **F** : water clarity problem.
- **FE** : Problem with the amount of water coming into your dishwasher. The solenoid valve is the cause.
- **HE** : Dishwasher heating circuit fault. This can be caused by the resistor, the klixon, the resistor wires or poor contact at the resistor terminals.
- **IE** : Water is not reaching the device.
- **LE** : problem related to the motor of your dishwasher.
- **OE** : Water is not being pumped or drained into your dishwasher.
- **PF** : A power outage has occurred.
- **TE** : heating problem.

For more information on these fault codes, do not hesitate to consult the websites of dishwasher manufacturers. If you have any questions, their FAQs will give you the answers. They also provide, for the most part, the dishwasher manuals, which are very useful if you have misplaced yours. If you do not know how to repair your dishwasher yourself and are unable to identify the origin of the fault, contact a specialist repairer. While waiting for their arrival, unplug your appliance and avoid using it.

How to renovate exposed beams?

Exposed wooden beams are a charming asset for an interior.

Exposed beams bring character and authenticity to the interior decoration of old buildings. Our advice for restoring them.

SUMMARY

- Check the condition of the beams
- How to achieve effective sanding?
- Sandblasting: a quick and ecological solution
- Applying the paint
- White lead: a refined finish

Used for centuries in construction , wooden beams have long been hidden under plaster ceilings or camouflaged behind modern coverings. Today, these architectural elements are very popular with interior decoration enthusiasts who see them as a warm and authentic way to embellish their home. Sanding, sandblasting, painting and whitewashing: here is the procedure to follow to enhance your exposed beams yourself.

Check the condition of the beams

Beyond their undeniable charm, it is essential to keep in mind that the beams maintain the structure of the building. Thus, their integrity is essential. Check for cracks, wood-eating insects, rot and deformation. If in doubt about the condition of the beams, the advice of a professional is strongly recommended.

Before beginning the restoration, remove the nails, staples and screws often present on these old pieces of wood using pliers or a screwdriver .

How to achieve effective sanding?

If your beams are relatively smooth or if there is a thin layer of paint , a simple sanding will be sufficient. To do this, make a first pass using medium-grit sandpaper (between 80 and 100) to remove imperfections, then a second pass with a finer grit (between 120 and 150) to refine the sanding. You can use an electric sander , especially if the surface to be sanded is large.

Sandblasting: a quick and ecological solution

Your beams may be covered with several layers of paint. In this case, it is possible to use a sandblaster or an aerogommeuse. The principle of this equipment is based on the projection of an abrasive propelled using a compressor. They are available for rental in specialized stores.

Highly effective, they allow for fast and environmentally friendly execution, without the use of harmful chemicals. Note that wearing protective glasses, a breathing mask and gloves is essential to ensure safe use of this equipment.

Applying the paint

Choose a woodwork paint whose tones match your interior decoration.

Here's how to do it:

1. Put on your protective equipment: masks, goggles and gloves.
2. Vacuum up any sanding or blasting residue to achieve a smooth surface.
3. Clean your exposed beams using a damp cloth .
4. Apply the paint in a thin layer, starting with the corners, and respecting the direction of the wood grain .
5. Proceed to the second coat, then a third if necessary.

White lead: a refined finish

It is a decorative technique used to highlight the grain of wood, by applying a light dye into the veins to create an elegant contrast.

The method for making a whitewash consists of:

- Dig out the pores by rubbing the beams in the direction of the wood with a wire brush.
- Remove brushing residue with a damp sponge .
- Apply a primer to block the tannins in the wood.
- Color the beams using whitewash paint.
- Remove excess paint.

How to renovate a straw chair?

Timeless and warm, straw chairs blend wonderfully with various interior decoration ambiances. Here's how to renovate them without resorting to the services of a re-seat.

SUMMARY

- **Can you renovate a straw chair yourself?**
- **Step 1: Sanding and cleaning the chair**
- **Step 2: Filling the holes and applying the varnish**
- **Step 3: Restoring the seat**

Often forgotten in attics or sold for a few euros in flea markets, straw chairs are nevertheless neglected treasures that regain their splendor once restored. With a limited budget and a little patience, it is possible to renovate them without having to face the difficulties of re-caning . What are the steps to follow to achieve this? Our advice.

Can you renovate a straw chair yourself ?

Mulching is far from being a simple technique. It requires training and skills. However, it is possible to create a new base using a much more accessible and less time-consuming method.

Here is the necessary material:

- foam board
- wooden board
- fabric
- varnish
- wood pulp
- wall stapler
- jigsaw
- brush
- sandpaper

Step 1: Sanding and cleaning the chair

They will help prepare the surface and thus facilitate the adhesion of the varnish to the wood.

1. Start by removing the mulch.
2. Sand the frame with coarse sandpaper , then finish with fine sandpaper to obtain a smooth surface.
3. Dust your antique chair carefully.
4. Then clean it with soapy water.
5. Rinse thoroughly to remove soap residue . This will prevent streaks from forming when applying the polish .

Step 2: Filling the holes and applying the varnish

Sometimes the ravages of time leave a few holes or cracks on old chairs. To remedy this, fill these imperfections with a little wood paste. Then, simply let it dry for the time indicated by the manufacturer and sand lightly to smooth the surface.

The choice of varnish will depend on your expectations in terms of finish. A matte product is perfect for preserving the raw appearance of the wood. Satin varnish is generally preferred for white wood, while glossy varnish is more suitable for dark wood.

Apply a first coat following the direction of the wood grain. Allow the recommended drying time before adding a second coat of varnish.

Step 3: Restoring the seat

While your varnish is drying, make your new seat. Proceed as follows:

- Collect the old mulch and use it as a template to trace its outline onto a sturdy wooden board. Then cut it out using a jigsaw.
- Draw and cut out this same model on the foam board.
- Wrap the board and foam with the fabric and attach it to the back of the seat with the wall stapler. Take care to pull the fabric well to avoid unwanted creases.
- Attach this seat to your newly renovated chair.

VMC making noise, what to do?

Purring, whistling... The ventilation system in your home is no longer very discreet. Why? How to react? How to proceed? Our answers.

SUMMARY

- Why is my VMC making a lot of noise?
- How can I spot a fault in my VMC installation and what should I do?
- How often should a VMC be maintained?

Can't stand the constant hum of your **controlled mechanical ventilation (CMV)** any longer ? This mechanism is essential to the quality of the ambient air in your home. Find out how to identify the causes of this noise and the solutions to remedy it. Also take advantage of some CMV maintenance tips to avoid noise pollution.

Why is my VMC making a lot of noise?

A single-flow or double-flow CMV (controlled mechanical ventilation) can be noisy for several reasons. This noise, often perceived as a hum or whistle, is generally due to vibrations and indicates a malfunction of the device.

The main causes of this problem are usually due to:

- **Lack of maintenance:** Over time, dirt and dust build up in the VMC ducts, clogging the system. Clean your ventilation at least once a year to remove these residues and avoid unwanted noise.
- **Incorrect air flow adjustment:** if the air flow is too powerful in relation to the size of the room, noise pollution may occur, even without intervention on the device.
- **A poorly positioned motor** : If the motor is poorly installed, often in false ceilings or attics , or if it is defective due to wear, strange noises can occur.
- **A VMC that is too old and worn** .

To remedy a noisy CMV, several actions can be taken depending on your diagnosis:

- lower the air flow

- replace the engine if it breaks down
- reattach and rebalance the engine if it is poorly positioned
- change the length of the sheaths
- change or replace worn sheaths, etc.

These interventions will reduce noise pollution and ensure the proper functioning of your VMC.

How can I spot a fault in my VMC installation and what should I do?

Start by checking the condition of your device and the equipment that makes it up: turbines, ducts, various air inlets and extraction box inlets.

To identify installation faults:

1. **Review the installation of the ducts** to check that they connect the VMC box to the distribution grilles as directly as possible.
2. **Adjust the diameter of the ducts** to avoid whistling and reduce the speed of the distributed air. Air circulation in the ventilation ducts must be at a maximum speed of 5 m/s for vertical ducts and 6 m/s for horizontal ducts. This optimal speed is obtained by using ventilation ducts with the appropriate diameter. Ducts that are too tight and/or multiple bends can generate excess decibels. They must connect the VMC box to the distribution grilles in a direct and natural manner. A duct diameter that is too small can create an unpleasant whistling sound.
3. **Check the position of the VMC box** . It is often installed directly on the attic floor or near a ventilation outlet. When in operation, the natural vibrations of the rotating elements are amplified and propagate through the ventilation ducts to

the ventilated rooms. This problem can be solved by installing anti-vibration pads between the device and the floor, or by suspending the box in the void between several frame elements. The VMC box must occupy a central position in the attic, equidistant from the various ventilation outlets that it irrigates.

4. **Consider installing noise-reducing devices** to block ventilation decibels: insulating box to be placed around the VMC motor, soundproof air extraction vents, VMC duct silencers to be placed on the ventilation duct sections to reduce the propagation of acoustic waves, etc.

This way, you can minimize the noise pollution from your VMC.

How often should a VMC be maintained?

Taking care of your VMC ensures its proper functioning and optimizes its performance. Not only do you extend its lifespan, but you also reduce your heating consumption ([1] energy saving) and limit the risks of humidity .

Here are some steps to take for regular maintenance :

- **Every 3 to 6 months:** clean the extraction and insufflation vents. Dismantle them, wash them with water and a degreasing product (such as dishwashing liquid) and let them dry before reattaching them. Also dust the air inlets with a vacuum cleaner.
- **Once a year:** check the filters of your VMC. If necessary, replace them or clean them with a degreasing product. Check the heat exchanger if you have a double-flow VMC.

---

1. http://www.lefigaro.fr/maison/chauffage-a-190c-obligation-recommandation-que-dit-la-loi-20231218

- **Every 2 to 3 years:** perform a complete system check, including cleaning the ducts and ducts.

Call an RGE professional (heating, refrigeration, electrician) for a complete maintenance of the VMC ideally in spring or autumn. He will thoroughly clean the ventilation circuits, maintain the ducts and the engine block, and check the fresh air inlets and the ventilation ducts.

It is entirely possible to minimize the noise pollution of your VMC. Don't forget to regularly clean the components of your VMC and to call a professional for a complete maintenance every 2 to 3 years. This way, you will enjoy a healthy and comfortable environment without being bothered by the noise of your ventilation system.

How to modernize paneling?

You no longer like the old paneling in your interior? For many reasons, it may be useful to keep it. But you can transform it. Stain, paint, wall covering... discover our tips.

SUMMARY

- **Why keep a paneled wall or ceiling in your home?**
- **5 tips for modernizing paneling**

Paneling, very popular in the 80s for its ability to cover walls and ceilings at low cost , is making a strong comeback in our interiors. It offers many advantages: durability and solidity, sound and thermal insulation, camouflage of damaged walls, etc.

If you no longer like the paneling in your living room, you should know that it can be easily modernized to match the decor of your home, transforming a cheesy element into a real charming asset.

Why keep a paneled wall or ceiling in your home?

Paneling has many benefits, both practical and aesthetic. Here's why it's a good idea to keep it or install it in your home.

- Paneling is **an excellent insulator**, both thermal and sound. It helps keep heat inside by reducing heat loss. It also protects against the cold and bad weather when used on the ceiling. In terms of sound insulation, paneling can reduce noise coming from adjoining walls and partitions, thus improving the acoustic comfort of your home.

- It is ideal for **hiding imperfections** and irregularities in walls. Rather than having to coat and sand to obtain an impeccable finish, paneling allows you to hide damaged supports in a simple and aesthetic way. It can be installed directly or on a frame with wooden battens, depending on the condition of the support.

- Paneling is a popular interior **design** element. It comes in different types of wood and finishes: rustic with dark or raw wood, country chic with whitewashed or bleached wood, classic with medium or light wood, and contemporary with painted wood. It can be easily customized with a coat of paint, to match all tastes and decorating styles.

- The paneling **adapts to all supports** and can be used in many configurations. Available in several materials such as wood, PVC and aluminum,[1] it offers great flexibility to adapt to your needs and your budget. Wood is aesthetic and durable, PVC is resistant and maintenance-free, and aluminum is the most robust, but also the most expensive.

- Easy to install, panelling is **perfect for low-cost interior**

---

1. http://www.lefigaro.fr/jardin/4-facons-d-utiliser-l-aluminium-au-jardin-20240417

makeovers . It can be quickly modified with a lick of paint to freshen up its appearance. In addition, it is durable and resistant, making it a practical material for all rooms in the house, including wet rooms if treated accordingly.

- Finally, wood paneling is an **ecological material** that can be recycled. Its solidity ensures good durability over time and its maintenance remains simple. Opting for paintable wood paneling allows you to change the color according to your desires without replacing the coating, thus contributing to a sustainable and environmentally friendly decoration.

5 tips for modernizing paneling

Even if you don't like your paneling anymore, it may be better to renovate it rather than remove it. Not only do you not know what you'll find underneath, but it may also require redoing the insulation in your room. Here are some tips for modernizing your paneling.

1. Use stain

Stain is a product that protects wood from stains and water while maintaining its natural appearance. It is durable and requires maintenance every 3 to 5 years. Our advice: use a water-based stain, which does not release toxic substances.

On well-dusted raw wood, apply one or two coats of stain. If the paneling has old finishes, light sanding is necessary. A colorless stain protects without changing the color of the wood, while a tinted stain, such as white, brings softness and modernizes the paneling.

2. Paint the paneling

Painting the paneling is a quick solution to modernize it.

- On raw paneling, the paint is applied directly.

- If the paneling is already painted, varnished or stained, sanding is necessary.
- For waxed or oiled paneling, sand until you get back to the raw wood and then degrease.

Use colored or white paints for a modern effect. Play with colors by creating patterns or friezes to energize the room, especially in a child's room . Treat yourself.

3. Cover the paneling with wall covering

For a radical transformation while keeping the paneling, you can cover it:

- Wallpaper : Choose original patterns to add texture and character to the room .[2]
- Fabric wall covering: Attach a durable, attractive fabric with glue or staples to create a sleek, solid wall.
- Adhesive tiles: PVC wall products offer a variety of shapes and colors, for a different decoration. They are also insulating.

4. Wax the paneling

Whitewashing is a technique that highlights the grain of the wood. Although long and tedious, it gives a unique and elegant appearance to the paneling slats.

Strip the wood completely, then use a wire brush to bring out the grain. Apply the whitewash and sand with coarse sandpaper. Finally, polish the wood or protect it with a colorless wax.

---

2. http://www.lefigaro.fr/maison/comment-reussir-la-pose-de-son-papier-peint-20230824

5. Apply a whitewash

A whitewash recreates the patina of bleached or aged wood, leaving the wood grain and marks visible. Protect surrounding surfaces, lightly sand walls, and clean off sanding residue. Prepare the whitewash according to directions and apply it with a brush or sponge following the grain of the wood. Wipe away traces to achieve the desired effect.

Modernizing paneling can completely transform the look of your home without the need for major renovations. Whether it's with stain, paint, wall coverings, whitewash or whitewash, these tips will give your paneling a new lease of life in an aesthetic and practical way.

Heat pump: should it be turned off when the good weather returns?

The heat pump has proven to be an efficient and economical way to heat your home. But with the arrival of the nice weather, a question arises: should you turn off the heat pump during warmer periods?

SUMMARY

- Should you stop a heat pump?
- How does a heat pump work?
- The right thing to do to preserve your heat pump

You have opted for a heat pump for your heating , or even your hot water production. But with summer coming, you are wondering if you should turn off your heat pump to save on your electricity bill. The answer in our article.

Should you stop a heat pump?

On sunny days, **turning off your heat pump is not recommended** . Logically, you won't do it if you have a reversible model that cools the rooms in the summer , or if it also produces hot water. But what about other models?

On a simple heat pump, restarting your device is more energy-intensive than leaving it on standby all summer. If, as a bonus, you restart your heat pump in the event of a cooling surge, starting it up cancels out all the benefits obtained.

In addition, a prolonged shutdown risks damaging 2 essential elements: the refrigerant and the compressor. The latter runs on oil, and stopping it for a long period of time clogs it and harms its proper functioning.

How does a heat pump work?

Note that there are 3 types of heat pumps. The first two, geothermal (ground-water heat pump) and hydrothermal (water-water heat pump), use calories from the ground and from groundwater respectively. We will focus on the most common, the aerothermal heat pump, or air-air or air-water heat pump.

Concretely, it captures the calories present in the air, then transmits them to a heat transfer fluid or refrigerant. The liquid is charged with heat and transformed into gas thanks to a compressor. It is then distributed:

- in radiators or heated floors for an air-water heat pump

- in heating ducts or wall consoles/splits for air-air heat pumps. This model is generally reversible: in cooling mode, the hot air from the home is then conducted out of the house by reversing the circuit.

If you do not have a reversible model, install wall-mounted air conditioning for the summer by following our installation advice.

The right thing to do to preserve your heat pump

Rising temperatures are the perfect time to discover the standby function of your heat pump. This mode is activated when the set temperature (usually between 12° and 16°C) is reached: no need to touch your heat pump, it manages itself.

Note that some models offer a summer mode, also based on autonomy. Your heat pump does not turn off completely, and thus its operation is preserved. Finally, connected thermostats in the rooms allow you to effectively regulate the temperature and leave your heating device on standby.

Once every two years, note in your diary the mandatory visit by a professional (decree no. 2020-912 of July 28, 2020). In addition to sealing and pressure control, he will check the standby settings with you.

And of course, installing a heat pump is combined with efficient insulation of your home: you are thus assured of optimal comfort at home.

How to paint a cinder block wall?

Strong but unsightly, the concrete block wall is transformed once repainted. Discover our guide to make it attractive and warm without the inconvenience of complex work.

SUMMARY

- Why paint a concrete block wall?
- What paint can be used?
- What equipment do you use to paint concrete blocks?
- Repaint a cinder block wall in 3 steps

Painting a concrete block wall is a simple and effective way to hide its roughness without the hassle of tedious and expensive rendering . What paint and what equipment should be used to meet the specific requirements of these concrete blocks ? How should you proceed to ensure uniform coverage?

Why paint a concrete block wall?

It must be admitted that in its raw state, this building material is not very aesthetic. Made up of cement, sand and gravel, its rough and dull appearance leaves an impression of coldness, even of unfinished work . The application of paint will transform this insipid surface into a welcoming and more personal decor.

Cinder block is a material that stands out for its porous texture. By covering it with paint, it will act as a protective barrier, which will limit the absorption of water.

What paint can be used?

The irregularity of the concrete block and its porosity make this material difficult to paint. It is therefore essential to choose a paint that is covering and resistant to humidity .[1] You can therefore turn to a single-coat facade paint that has these two characteristics.

There are also paints specially designed to cover concrete blocks. Their dense formulation and high viscosity perfectly meet the requirements of this support.

What equipment do you use to paint concrete blocks?

You will need the following materials:

- sprayer
- long pile roller
- facade cleaner
- facade coating, plastering knife, trowel and sander (optional)
- undercoat paint
- single-coat paint for facade or special paint for concrete blocks

---

1. http://www.lefigaro.fr/maison/comment-chassez-l-humidite-d-une-maison-20240510

Repaint a cinder block wall in 3 steps

Step 1: Preparing the surface

Your wall must be free of any dirt to ensure the paint adheres . If its construction is several years old, it is advisable to remove the impurities using a facade cleaner.

Proceed as follows:

- Dilute the product according to the recommended dosages.
- Apply the cleaner using a sprayer. You can brush the dirtiest areas.
- Leave to act according to the manufacturer's recommendations.
- Rinse thoroughly with water.

If the support has cracks or holes , you will need to fill them with filler. Use the following method:

- Fill cracks and holes with filler.
- Smooth with a trowel.
- Allow to dry for the time recommended by the manufacturer.
- Sand to even out the surface.

Step 2: Laying the underlay

Although this step is optional, it is highly recommended. The undercoat will help the paint adhere. Its covering power also reduces the number of coats of paint needed.

Here's how to do it: Clear the corners using a sash brush , then apply the undercoat with a roller, starting at the top of the wall. Finally, let it dry for the required time.

Step 3: Applying the paint

Proceed in the same way as for laying the undercoat. Always make sure to respect the drying times between each coat if several are necessary

My window no longer opens: what are the solutions?

When it no longer opens, a window can quickly become a source of frustration. However, this joinery does not systematically need to be replaced.

SUMMARY

- **Why is my window stuck?**
- **What solutions are there for unlocking a window?**
- **How to force a stuck window?**

With a simple gesture, we ventilate and cool our home by opening the windows . But when these windows are blocked, all the comfort of our daily lives is compromised. What are the causes of this malfunction and what can be done to fix it? Our tips for finding a well-ventilated home.

Why is my window stuck?

There are several factors that can cause this problem:

- A malfunction of the handle is sometimes responsible for this blockage.
- If your carpentry is equipped with a lock , it can be damaged, especially if you use it frequently.
- Hinges can also come loose, especially if you live on a sloping lot .
- Weather- related material deformation can also cause this problem if your window is made of PVC or wood. PVC can expand due to temperature variations. Being sensitive to humidity ,[1] wood also tends to swell.

What solutions are there for unlocking a window?

Before considering replacing your window, you can try these methods. If you are not comfortable with these interventions, call a professional. Improper handling could make the problem worse or even be detrimental to your woodwork.

After identifying the reason for the blockage, try these solutions to resolve the issue:

- If the blockage is due to the handle, you will need to disassemble it. To do this, unscrew the screws that secure it. Check the components and replace them if necessary.
- Lubricate the lock if you have noticed a malfunction in the mechanism or key .[2] If this solution does not work, disassemble it and replace it.
- Tighten the hinges with a screwdriver if you suspect these components are causing the jamming.

---

1. http://www.lefigaro.fr/maison/comment-chassez-l-humidite-d-une-maison-20240510

2. http://www.lefigaro.fr/maison/j-ai-perdu-mes-cles-que-puis-je-faire-20230215

- If your wooden window has swollen due to humidity, it is possible to sand down the parts that rub or get stuck. Be careful not to remove too much material, because when the humidity has disappeared, the woodwork will return to its original shape.

How to force a stuck window?

These 4 tips may help you overcome your blocked window. Be careful, these methods can damage your woodwork. If in doubt, seek professional help.

Tip #1: Use a crowbar

Place the tool between the window frame and the window sash, and apply light pressure. Use caution to avoid damaging the frame or mechanism.

Tip #2: Dehumidify the wood

If your window blockage is related to moisture, you can dry the edges of the frame with a hair dryer. Using a dehumidifier in the room can also work.

Tip #3: Saw off the hinges

As a last resort, you can saw off the window hinges. However, this radical method risks significantly damaging the woodwork or even requiring its replacement.

My refrigerator is making ice: causes and solutions

If your refrigerator is constantly covered in ice despite frequent defrosting, it is possible that this problem is the result of an underlying malfunction. What are the possible reasons for the formation of ice? What are the ways to remove frost?

SUMMARY

- Possible causes of frost build-up
- Steps to Remove Ice from the Refrigerator

Loss of energy efficiency of the appliance, deterioration of food storage conditions , risks of breakdown: the accumulation of ice in a refrigerator can be the cause of significant inconvenience. To resolve this problem, identification of the underlying cause is necessary.

Possible causes of frost build-up

The temperature is incorrectly set or the thermostat is

defective

When the thermostat is set too low or if it is defective, ice may form on the walls of the appliance. You can increase it slightly if you notice excessive ice.

The room is too hot

Your appliance belongs to a climate class. This indicates that it is designed to operate when the temperature is within a defined range, for example between 16 and 32 °C for the temperate climate class (N).

If the ambient temperature exceeds this range, the refrigerator may not be able to function optimally, which can lead to excessive frost production. Be careful of the presence of radiators or an oven nearby, which can also contribute to the increase in ambient temperature.

The refrigerator is too full

Too much food in the appliance will prevent air circulation. This can create an uneven temperature distribution with colder, potentially frozen, areas.

The door seal is no longer airtight

If the door no longer closes properly, warmer air from the room will enter the appliance. It will then condense on contact with the cold and produce ice on the walls.

The light switch no longer works

A working lamp produces heat. If it remains lit when the door is closed, this heat will generate condensation, then frost.

The fan is broken

If this essential component fails, cold air will no longer circulate through the appliance, causing ice to build up in the coldest areas.

Steps to Remove Ice from the Refrigerator

Here's how to defrost your appliance in 4 steps.

Step 1: Food removal

Remove all food from inside the appliance. You can store it in a cooler to keep it cool while defrosting.

Step 2: Preparing the refrigerator

Unplug the appliance to stop the system from cooling. Place towels or mops around the refrigerator to prevent water from flowing into the room.

Step 3: Defrosting

Then defrost using a scraper or wooden spatula. You can use these 3 methods to speed up the process:

- Place a basin of hot water inside the appliance.
- Heat the frosted wall with a hair dryer. For safety, make sure to maintain a minimum distance of 30 cm.
- Use a commercially available de-icing spray.

Step 4: Recommissioning

Clean the defrosted refrigerator with a mixture of water and white vinegar. Plug the appliance back in and put the food back inside.

The air from my air conditioning smells bad, what should I do?

Stale air, foul odor: air conditioners can cause unpleasant odors. To solve this problem, discover the cause of odors and our tips for remedying them.

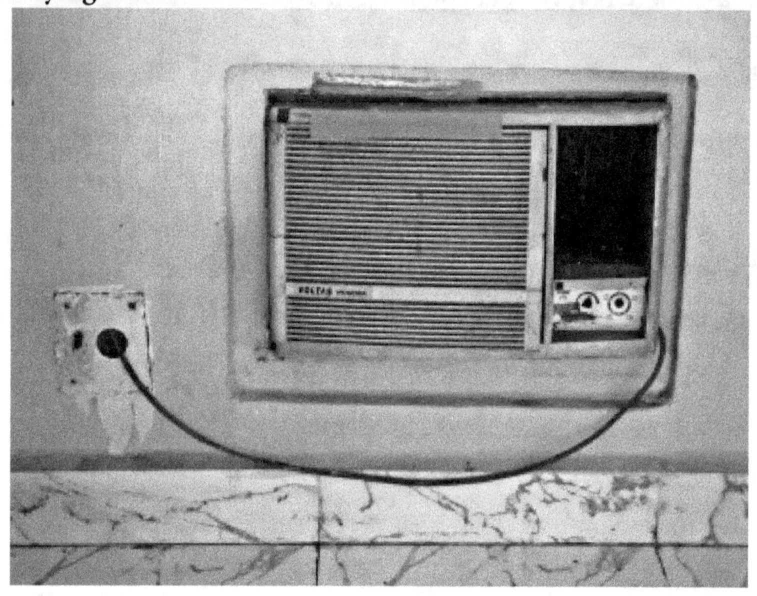

SUMMARY

- **Why does my home air conditioning smell bad?**
- **How to fight bad odors?**

Have you noticed that your **air conditioning** is giving off an unpleasant odor ? The smell of damp laundry or rotten eggs may indicate a lack of maintenance. Discover the possible causes of these bad odors and the solutions to eliminate them, in order to regain healthy and pleasant air in your home.

Why does my home air conditioning smell bad?

Bad odors released by your air conditioning generally come from a lack of maintenance or cleaning . Several factors can be responsible for these unpleasant odors:

1. **Lack of filter maintenance:** A clogged filter can be a source of bad odors. Also, clean your air conditioning filters regularly to avoid the accumulation of dust , bacteria and mold that can cause these foul odors.

2. **Mold and mildew:** If you smell a musty or moldy odor, your air conditioning system is likely infested with mold, mildew, or bacteria. Moisture in the cooling system can create condensation ,[1] which can help these pathogens grow. Areas to monitor include the coils, evaporator, air ducts, ductwork, filter, and condensate pan.

3. **Indoor humidity** : poor condensate drainage, especially without a siphon, can lead to water accumulation. This stagnant water becomes a breeding ground for bacteria and mold, giving off a damp or damp smell. Make sure the condensate drainage is working properly and is not blocked.

4. **The presence of a dead animal** : A rotten egg or sewer smell may indicate the presence of a small dead animal that has entered the ventilation duct. Quickly remove any dead insect or rodent to eliminate the bad smell.

5. **Refrigerant gas leak** : Although rare, a refrigerant gas leak can also cause a bad smell. This situation requires immediate intervention by a professional to diagnose and repair the leak.

---

1. http://www.lefigaro.fr/maison/comment-eviter-la-condensation-sur-les-vitres-de-la-maison-20240412

How to fight bad odors?

Bad odors from your air conditioning can often be eliminated with a thorough cleaning and regular maintenance of your unit. Concretely, what should you clean?

1. Filters

There are two types of filters for air conditioners: activated carbon filters and mechanical filters.

     ● ***Activated carbon filters*** are responsible for filtering odors. They must be replaced twice a year. If your air conditioning gives off an unpleasant odor, the first thing to do is to check the condition of the carbon filter. Unlike mechanical filters, carbon filters cannot be cleaned, they must be changed. To replace them: open the hood of your air conditioner, remove and throw away the used carbon filter. Then place a new activated carbon filter.

     ● ***Mechanical or electrostatic filters*** capture bacteria, dust, and pollen . They should be cleaned regularly, about twice a month. Remove the mechanical filters, vacuum up the accumulated dust. Clean them with soapy water, a baking soda solution , or a disinfectant if you notice mold. Let the filters dry completely before replacing them.

2. The condensate tray

The condensate pan collects water from the humidity generated by the air conditioner. A dirty or clogged pan can cause bad odors. To clean it, disconnect the drain hose. Remove the condensate pan and empty it into the toilet . Clean the pan with soapy water and a sponge . Dry it with a dry cloth , replace it and reconnect the drain hose. Check that it is draining properly by pouring a little water into the pan.

3. The condensate line

A clogged condensate line can also affect the performance of your air conditioner and cause unpleasant odors. Unplug your air conditioner to clean it. Remove the condensate hose and check for obstructions. If so, use a vacuum cleaner to remove the dirt. Clean the hose with a glass of bleach or an antibacterial product. Reconnect the condensate hose.

By following these steps, you should avoid bad odors coming from your air conditioning. Make sure to maintain it regularly to keep the air clean and pleasant in your home. If despite your efforts the bad odors persist, we advise you to call a professional. They will be able to accurately diagnose the source of the problem and carry out the necessary repairs for healthy air conditioning.

How to fix a TV to placo with a TV bracket attached to the wall?

To mount a wall-mounted TV on Placoplâtre, a fixed TV bracket is the easiest and safest solution. Especially if your TV is directly opposite your sofa or armchair, and you don't plan on changing the layout of your room. A fixed bracket keeps the TV close to the wall, eliminating the risk of it being pulled out thanks to the vertical force exerted on the fixing points.

To install this type of support on a placo wall, a few Molly-type metal anchors are sufficient.

- Start by mounting the plate on the back of the TV
- Secure the wall bracket using the Molly anchors.
- Secure the TV with the wall mount.

In general, it is not necessary to fix the bracket to the metal rails behind the BA13, except for the most massive TVs (weight over 40 kg).

A fixed TV mount is particularly suitable for large and heavy screens, offering more security than a swivel wall mount.

Can you use a tilting TV mount on Placoplâtre?

Do you want to install your TV at a certain height, and be able to tilt the screen downwards according to the configuration of your living room, for better visual comfort? Integrate a system with built-in or wall-mounted speakers? A tilting TV mount is the ideal choice, because it allows you to tilt the screen slightly downwards while minimizing the offset of the TV from the wall. The other advantage of a swivel and tilt mount is that it offers easy access to connections (HDMI, USB, RJ45, etc.). For large screens, a swivel mount is often the best option to combine safety and flexibility.

On the other hand, for TVs weighing more than 40 kilos, it is better to fix the TV bracket to metal rails or wooden rafters behind the placo, using metal dowels or lag screws. A TV wall bracket with an articulated arm, which allows you to orient and tilt your screen, is another option. This type of bracket offers a large anchoring surface, which improves resistance to tearing, especially for large screens from 37 to 84 inches.

How to fix a TV bracket with articulated arm on BA13?

Fixing a TV bracket with an articulated arm to Placoplâtre requires taking into account the limited resistance of BA13, especially when faced with the forces exerted by the offset arm.

Be aware that to install a tilting or swivel bracket for your television, reinforcing the wall is essential to prevent it from falling. There are three main solutions:

1- Fix it to the metal rails or wooden rafters that hold the plasterboard .

This method is best suited for wider TV brackets, as the spacing between the rails or rafters can be as much as 40 to 60 cm. To locate these structures, use a material detector or tap the wall to identify non-hollow areas. Although the strength of metal rails is greater than that of placo, it is still limited. Use metal dowels for the rails or lag screws for the rafters (after pre-drilling with a wood drill bit to avoid splitting).

2- Fix directly into the concrete block wall behind the plasterboard:

use threaded rods anchored into the concrete block, solid brick or stone wall, with a chemical seal. This solution guarantees a secure fixing, but requires DIY skills .

3- Reinforce the wall with a special heavy-duty plasterboard,

designed to support heavy loads on any type of wall with a standard metal frame.

In conclusion, to mount a television on a Placoplâtre wall, you must take precautions to ensure a secure installation. If you want to use a tilting or swivel mount, consider reinforcing the wall or anchoring the mount in a solid structure behind the placo. Also favor Molly anchors and fixed brackets for optimal stability, especially for heavy screens. By following these tips, you will be able to enjoy your television without the risk of it falling or damaging your wall.

How to hide exposed radiator pipes?

Painting, formwork, gutters and cornices are all solutions to no longer see the long, unsightly tubes of the heating system. Discover our best tips.

SUMMARY

- Create custom formwork
- Installing gutters and cornices
- Painting the pipes

Exposed radiator pipes often represent a challenge when you want to decorate your home. They are certainly essential for heating and plumbing , but they can degrade the aesthetics of a room. Fortunately, various solutions exist to cleverly conceal them and integrate them harmoniously into your design. From discreet casings to clever decorative elements, discover the best techniques to hide, or even enhance, these radiator pipes.

Create custom formwork

To hide unsightly radiator pipes and taps visible in your home, creating a custom casing has many advantages. In addition to the aesthetic aspect, such a device protects the pipes and facilitates cleaning by preventing the accumulation of dust .

What material for the formwork?

Different materials can be used to make formwork, such as:

- Plywood or solid wood (oak, paneling, MDF, water-repellent chipboard, etc.)
- Plasterboard (plasterboard)[1]
- Plastic.

Each of these materials has specific advantages for their ease of handling, resistance to humidity and their aesthetic appeal. Choose a material that meets your aesthetic and functional needs, while taking into account the specific constraints of your interior space.

How to make formwork yourself ?

The manufacture of custom formwork involves several steps.

---

1. http://www.lefigaro.fr/maison/comment-faire-et-utiliser-du-platre-20220921

1. First, take precise measurements of the space where you want to embed the wall formwork, taking into account the size of the pipes and the available space.
2. Cut the selected material to the desired dimensions using suitable tools , such as a jigsaw or hole saw.
3. Then secure the formwork boards or panels using cleats, making sure to leave sufficient space between the pipes and the cleats to avoid overheating.
4. Finally, finish the formwork by adding finishes such as paint ,[2] tiles or the covering of your choice so that it blends harmoniously into your interior space.

Don't forget to ensure accessibility when cutting: integrate an inspection hatch into the formwork to allow easy access to the pipes and the tap to access the water supply if necessary. This hatch should be easily removable to facilitate any repairs or work on the pipes. Also ensure that valves and taps are accessible through air vents or access hatches to avoid any difficulty when using or maintaining them. By ensuring adequate accessibility, you ensure that your formwork remains functional and practical in the long term.

If you are a handyman , you can also fit a small piece of furniture or shelves to create storage around your hidden pipes.

Installing decorative trunking and cornices to conceal exposed radiator pipework in the home is an aesthetic and practical solution.

Trunking, similar to electrical wire covers but more elegant, is placed around the pipes and can be easily removed thanks to its sliding or clip-on system. This method allows quick access to the pipes when needed, while facilitating maintenance. Available in a wide range of models, the plastic or PVC trunking and cornice offer different shapes and colours to adapt to the aesthetics of your interior. Measure the

---

2. http://www.lefigaro.fr/maison/quelles-peintures-choisir-pour-repeindre-son-interieur-20230115

diameter of the pipes carefully before purchasing to ensure an optimal fit of the conduits.

PVC cornices , for their part, are perfectly suited as a high pipe cover and are easily attached to the edges of the pipe supports. Decorative and removable, they allow quick access to the conduits while maintaining a neat aesthetic.

Easily found in DIY stores , trunking and cornices come in standard sizes and can also be used to conceal pipes.

Finally, also think about hiding the pipes close to the ground with a wooden, PVC or tiled skirting board called a surplinth.

Painting the pipes

Painting the pipes against the wall remains the quickest and cheapest decorative method to hide exposed radiator pipes in the house. A simple option is to paint them the same color as the wall , which allows them to blend discreetly into the decor. This tone-on-tone paint allows you to obtain a discreet and harmonious result.

For those who prefer a more daring approach, color contrast can be an interesting option. By painting the pipes with a bright, warm color, in total contrast to the ambient color, you create a striking decorative effect that highlights the network of pipes. This technique brings a touch of dynamism to the space, creating a vitamin effect.

Another elegant option is to paint all the pipes black or dark paint, which gives them a sober and discreet presence. Black contrasts harmoniously with many noble materials and brings a touch of elegance to the whole.

Squeaky Bed: 5 Solutions to Make It Quiet

There's nothing more annoying than the constant creaking of a bed that disrupts your sleep. Whether the problem comes from your box spring, your mattress or the bed frame, here are five effective tips to help you get back to sleep with peace of mind.

SUMMARY

- Lubricate the box spring
- Turn the mattress over
- Tighten and grease the bed frame screws
- Glue pads under the bed legs
- Seal the gaps between the box spring and the frame

Getting restful sleep is important for our body, our mind, our health. Having good bedding helps with this. If your bed creaks, there are simple solutions to remedy this problem and regain peaceful nights.

Lubricate the box spring

Bed squeaks can come from the box spring, especially if you have a slatted or box spring. The slats can rub against the bed posts, while the springs can deteriorate over time, creating annoying noises.

To remedy these squeaks, check that the noises are indeed coming from your box spring and apply the correct lubrication methods:

- If your box spring is made of wood or metal and parts touch, you can apply soap,[1] talcum powder, beeswax or graphite powder to the joints to reduce friction and eliminate noise.
- For box springs, where squeaking is less common thanks to pocket spring technology, check the condition of the outer springs and apply a little oil if necessary to reduce any possible noise.

Finally, make sure your box spring fits properly into the frame and headboard to avoid squeaking due to misalignment.

IMPROVE YOUR SLEEP WITH TEDIBER

Turn the mattress over

When your bed squeaks, the culprit may be the mattress , especially if it has springs. To check, lay it on the floor and roll around on it. If you hear squeaking, the problem is with the mattress. This can also happen with memory foam mattresses.

---

1. http://www.lefigaro.fr/maison/8-utilisations-du-savon-noir-a-la-maison-20230403

First, try turning the mattress. This will redistribute your body weight and reduce noise. Ideally, you should turn your spring mattress every six months or so to prevent wear and tear from your body weight. This will help preserve the quality of the mattress and reduce squeaking.

If the noises persist, make sure the mattress is properly aligned on the box spring or inserted correctly into the bed frame.

Tighten and grease the bed frame screws

Is the problem not coming from your box spring or your mattress? What if it comes from the bed frame itself? To determine the origin of the noises, carefully inspect the tightness of the screws and bolts.

- If any screws are loose, take the time to adjust them properly. Using an Allen key and a screwdriver, tighten the bolts and frame parts that are loose. Focus especially on the corners of the frame, where the noises are often the most pronounced. Then check if the squeaking has stopped.
- If the screws are rusty, it is better to replace them to ensure the stability of the structure.

If the noises persist, make sure that all frame parts are properly aligned and that the fixings are solid.

Glue pads under the bed legs

A squeaky bed can also sometimes indicate a stability problem caused by a difference in the size of the bed legs or a bedroom floor that is not perfectly flat. To remedy this:

- Start by removing the mattress and box spring to access the feet of the bed.
- Next, place non-slip pads or glides under each leg to

compensate for uneven floors and ensure better stability. You can find these accessories in DIY stores, where they are usually available in the hardware section.

Whether you opt for anti-slip pads or glides, make sure to choose durable models. These accessories are also useful for other furniture in the house, such as chairs, sofas or desks, to prevent scratches on the floor and ensure better stability.

Seal the gaps between the box spring and the frame

The last possibility to explain why your bed creaks: there may be too many spaces between the wooden plates of the bed base or the joints of the bed. To solve this problem, several simple solutions can be considered.

- If there are gaps between the wooden boards of the bed base, you can fill them with pieces of cork. These small pieces of padding will help to tighten the parts of the bed that make noise.

- To reduce the squeaking caused by the contact of the wood of the slats against the metal of the bed base, you can use different substances such as talcum powder, wax or petroleum jelly. Applying talcum powder to the joints will reduce friction and therefore noise. Candle wax can also be used by pouring it on the joints to eliminate unwanted noise. Similarly, applying petroleum jelly or glycerin to the joints will lubricate the parts of the bed and prevent them from squeaking.

By following these simple tips, you are now ready to get back to a restful and squeak-free sleep. If despite everything, the problem persists, do not hesitate to consider purchasing a bed with box spring and mattress for quality sleep.

Tips for hiding electrical wires in your home

Unsightly and cumbersome, electrical wires may run along the walls of your home. If you only see them, don't despair! Here are our solutions to hide them.

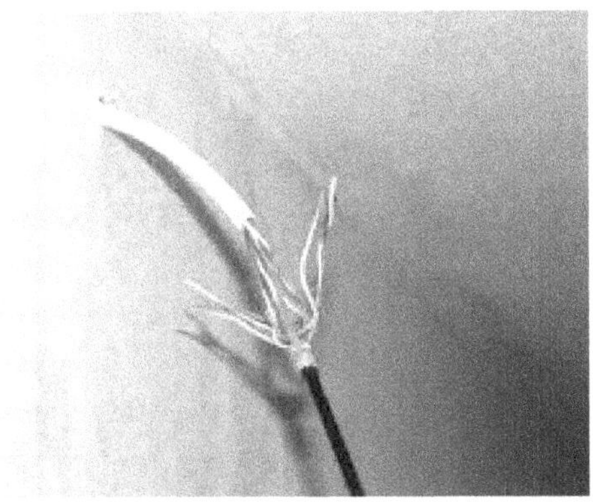

The presence of a few exposed electrical wires is enough to ruin the most successful interior decoration. However, with a little creativity and ingenuity, it is possible to cleverly camouflage this messy tangle. DIYer or not, we present six simple and practical tips to hide the electrical wires in the house.

A conventional method: the electric chute

A cable duct is a plastic or metal box attached to a wall or ceiling, designed to conceal electrical wires and cables. There are many models available in a variety of sizes and colors.

Electric baseboards: the most discreet approach

It is actually a skirting board with a space for integrating electrical wires. With it, you will finalize the decoration of your room, but you will also effectively hide unsightly cables. Unlike the trunking, it is only installed at the bottom of the wall .

The electric skirting board is the most discreet solution for hiding electrical wires, as it fits perfectly into the decor of the room. Its installation does not require major work .

Simple and effective: the storage box

If you can't stand tangled cables under your desk or behind your TV, a storage box will help you solve this mess. In addition to being aesthetic, this device will accommodate your power strips and keep your electrical equipment out of reach of children and pets .[1] You will find storage boxes in various sizes and materials.

Masking tape: an economical tip

This masking tape, straight from Japan, lends itself to all sorts of decorative and practical uses. Instead of hiding your wires, you will dress them in pretty colors that match the ambiance of your room. Masking tape is the most economical choice to personalize and embellish your electrical wires.

The rope: to free your creativity

By making a cord cover with rope, you will bring a touch of nature to your decoration. You can also hide your cords in an original way

---

1. http://www.lefigaro.fr/animaux/animaux-de-compagnie-quels-sont-les-accidents-domestiques-les-plus-frequents-20221122

by using macramé techniques. This material is very popular for its bohemian look.

Wall lining: a radical solution

As the name suggests, this trick involves creating an additional wall. For example, you could opt for a wooden wall that would bring a little warmth to a room that is considered too impersonal. Doubling a wall is also a great way to demarcate a space, such as an office corner or a reading area

How to hide your electric meter?

Electricity meters, both new and old ones, are not known for their appearance. There are ways to hide them to have a more harmonious interior.

SUMMARY

- **Integrating the electric meter into a piece of furniture**
- **Make a wooden formwork**
- **Other tips for hiding the electric meter**

Although essential, **electric meters** are often unsightly. Fortunately, there are many tricks to camouflage them while beautifying your interior. Whether by hiding them behind a decorative panel or by integrating them into a piece of furniture , you can transform this equipment into an asset for your decoration. Discover how to hide your electric meter without sacrificing accessibility or style.

Integrating the electric meter into a piece of furniture

Integrating the electric meter into a piece of furniture allows it to be hidden while maintaining easy access. This method allows both the meter and the electrical panel to be hidden, thus facilitating access to the circuit breakers and the reading of energy consumption (and establishing your electricity bill) without requiring complex work .

Depending on the location of the meter and the space available, several furniture options are available to you.

- In an entrance hall, you can opt for a shoe cabinet, a closet with hanging space or a key box .
- In a hallway, a wall unit or a narrow cupboard may be suitable.
- In the living room or dining room, a sideboard or shelf can be a good solution, etc.

If ready-made furniture is not suitable, custom-made is an excellent alternative.

When installing, be careful not to fix the bottom of the cabinet to enclose the electric meter. Make sure that the meter remains easily accessible for readings from your electricity supplier and that the space is well ventilated to prevent any risk of overheating.

Make a wooden formwork

Building a wooden casing to hide an electric meter is an accessible DIY project that can improve the aesthetics of your interior while preserving the functionality of the electrical installation. To build it, you will need:

- Wooden boards (plywood or MDF)
- Hinges
- Wood screws
- Screwdriver or electric screwdriver
- Saw (jigsaw or circular)
- Tape measure
- Spirit level
- Pencil
- Square
- Sandpaper
- Paint or varnish (optional)

Here are the steps to achieve it:

1. Take the exact dimensions of the electricity meter, adding a few centimeters on each side for opening and ventilation .
2. Use a saw to cut the wooden boards to these dimensions. You will need four main panels (two for the sides, one for the top and one for the bottom) and a door for the front.
3. Sand the edges of the cut boards to remove splinters and achieve a smooth finish.
4. Assemble the four main formwork panels using wood screws. Use a square to ensure that the corners are square. Check that the structure is square using a spirit level and a square.
5. Attach the hinges to one side of the door and to the edge of one of the side panels of the formwork. Check that the door opens and closes properly. Adjust the hinges if necessary for perfect alignment.
6. Attach a small handle to the door to make it easier to open.
7. Place the formwork in front of the Linky meter and mark the points where you will fix the formwork to the wall. Drill holes in the wall using a drill and insert dowels if necessary.

Secure the formwork securely to the wall with screws.

To protect the wood and improve its aesthetics, apply a coat of paint or varnish. You can also cover it with decorative wallpaper , paint it the same color as the walls , or add stickers and other decorative elements according to your tastes.

Other tips for hiding the electric meter

Hiding a single-phase or three-phase electric meter does not necessarily require being an expert in carpentry or DIY. Here are some simple and effective ideas to hide your meter while adding an aesthetic touch to your interior. You can camouflage it behind:

- **A frame or poster** : Buy or make a small wooden box the exact size of your meter. Customize it with a poster or photos to add a personal touch.
- **A mirror** : hang it on the formwork, to take a look at your look before going out, but also to visually enlarge the room. This is particularly suitable for small spaces.
- **A wall-mounted key box** : transform the inside of your meter box into a key box to combine business with pleasure. You can also hang a few hooks underneath to hang your keys, umbrellas , etc.
- **A curtain or drapery** : Install a curtain or drapery in front of the meter to hide it from view. Make sure the fabric is at a sufficient distance to avoid any risk of incident.
- **A screen** : placed in front of the meter, it also adds a decorative touch to your room.
- **An access hatch** : if your meter is built into a wall or niche, use an access hatch to hide it. These hatches, often without a handle and opening with a simple push, are practical and

aesthetic.

- **A ready-to-install meter cover** : they come in different sizes and colours in DIY stores to dress up your meters.
- **Trompe l'oeil** : A creative option is to use paint, wallpaper or a trompe l'oeil sticker to create the illusion that the counter is another element in the room, such as a window, shelf or painting.

Whether you choose to integrate your meter into a piece of furniture, hide it behind a frame or use a wooden casing, there are many solutions available to you to camouflage your electric meter in an aesthetic and practical way. Let your creativity run wild to transform this essential but not very decorative element into an asset for your interior.

How to put up wallpaper without glue?

The Easy Roll process designed by Castorama is really very simple to implement, because it eliminates the chore of pasting the strips of wallpaper.

SUMMARY

- **How do I install this wallpaper without pasting?**
- **What equipment to use?**
- **Conclusion on installing wallpaper without glue**

Before starting, it is important to properly prepare the wall[1] on which the wallpaper will be placed. You cannot avoid removing the old wallpaper before sticking the new one. If the surface has irregularities, cracks or holes ,[2] you must apply a layer of plaster to fill them, and sand

---

1. http://www.lefigaro.fr/maison/dossier/preparer-reparer-et-peindre-un-mur-tous-nos-conseils

the excess material with sandpaper. The goal is to obtain a perfectly flat and smooth surface. Similarly, cleaning the dirt, by giving it a good wipe with a sponge and a scouring product, will increase the adhesion of the glue. Before starting, remember to stretch a protective tarpaulin at the foot of your wall to avoid soaking your floor. The water that you are going to spray may indeed leak.

How do I install this wallpaper without pasting?

1 Get off to a good start

Using a tape measure, mark several points 50 cm from the corner of the wall. The roll is 53 cm wide, so you will have some excess. Draw a horizontal line from the ceiling to the floor. This will serve as a guide for laying the first strip.

2 Spray water on the wall

Before cutting the first strip of wallpaper , remember to measure the required height and add 5 to 10 cm at each end. Using the spray bottle, generously spray the surface of your wall. For a 2.5 m long panel, Castorama recommends a water volume of between 500 and 600 ml, hence the importance of protecting your floor well! You can then lay the wallpaper following the mark you have previously drawn.

3. Squeeze out air bubbles under the paper

Once the first strip is perfectly aligned with your mark, you can start smoothing it down using a wallpaper brush. The aim is to get rid of any air pockets trapped during installation. Start from the centre of the strip of wallpaper and work your way down to the edges, brushing it downwards. Don't hesitate to peel the edges back off and add a

---

2. http://www.lefigaro.fr/maison/comment-reboucher-un-trou-dans-un-mur-20220805

few sprays of water if you have trouble getting rid of all the bubbles. You have about ten minutes to reposition the wallpaper before it dries completely.

Good to know

Do not hesitate to lift each edge of the strip to add water, in order to ensure the adhesion of the support.

3 Cut off the overhangs

When you are satisfied with the installation, you can start cutting off the excess paper. Use a cutter and a ruler to follow the angle of the ceiling and the line of the skirting board. Make sure the blade is new. Remember, if necessary, to wipe off any traces of water with a clean sponge. Before moving on to the next strip, check the connection of the patterns so that they are perfectly aligned with each other. Finally, cut off the excess on the corners, at each end of the wall. Take your time and be precise for this last operation.

A large choice

This collection is available in 36 patterns and colours. The 10 m long rolls (53 cm wide) are sold for €21.90 each (except the Bagatelle pink model, which costs €22.90).

What equipment to use?

- **The wallpaper brush.** This is an essential tool for hanging wallpaper. It is used for smoothing and removing air bubbles trapped between the wall and the strip. Expect to pay around ten euros to buy it.
- **The sprayer.** It allows water to be applied evenly to the wall. They come in different capacities. Expect to pay between €5

and €15.

- **The glue wheel.** This small tool (around €5) is used to flatten the edges of the strips on the wall (but also to remove small air bubbles) to make the joints as invisible as possible.
- **The cutter.** It is used to cut overhangs at corners, ceilings and skirting boards. Choose a model equipped with a blade reservoir (around twenty euros).

Conclusion on installing wallpaper without glue

The principle of this pre-pasted wallpaper is very interesting. The installation is really simpler, because it requires very little material and much less preparation than for classic rolls. It is also faster. However, it is necessary to protect your floor well before working, the water applied to the wall tends to flow. Ideal for decoration, to cover a single wall in a room.

Peeling paint: what to do?

Blistering or peeling paint can be caused by a number of factors such as humidity in the room, improper surface preparation or incompatibility between the paints used.

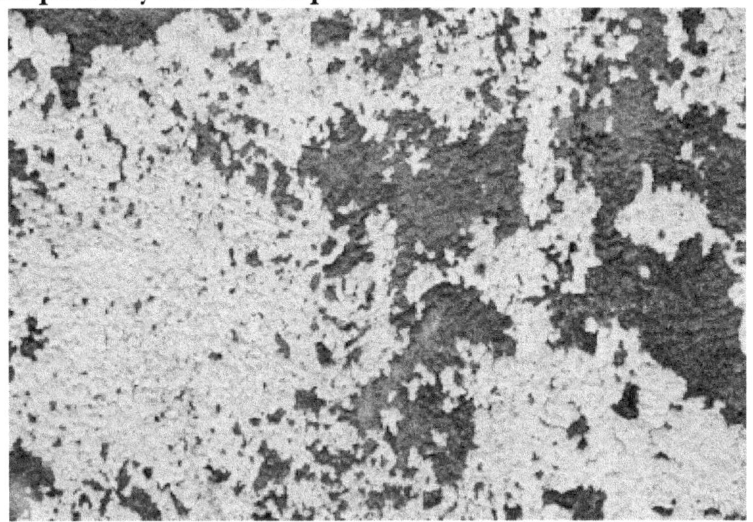

SUMMARY

- Why does paint blister or warp?
- How to remove air bubbles in paint?
- How to paint without blistering?

This defect results in the appearance of unsightly pockets or bubbles of paint . How to avoid blisters and how to repair paint that is warping on a wall or ceiling ?

Why does paint blister or warp?

The formation of blisters or warps on a paint can be caused by several factors, mainly related to humidity , but not only. Here are the main causes of blistering of a paint:

Moisture in the wall can cause blistering, especially if you are using a waterproof paint like oil-based paint. The moisture trapped in the paint tries to evaporate, creating blisters.

Incompatibility of paints such as using water-based paint over oil-based paint can cause problems as they are incompatible and can separate.

Painting a wall in weather that is too hot or too cold can also be problematic. A temperature between 15 and 25°C is recommended for optimal drying of the paint. Application in hot weather can cause the surface to dry too quickly, preventing the solvents from escaping from the core of the paint.

Failure to allow sufficient drying time between coats can cause blistering, as the top coat dries faster than the bottom coat, forming a barrier to water vapor.

Finally, a coat of paint that is too thick can prevent the solvents from evaporating, leading to blistering.

To remedy this problem, it is recommended to let the paint dry completely, then sand down the blistered areas. Then apply an undercoat with a brush, let dry and finish with a new coat of paint. For gloss or satin paints, it may be necessary to repaint the entire surface to avoid rework marks.

How to remove air bubbles in paint?

Step one: Identify the source of the problem in order to resolve it before starting the renovation work , as ignoring this step could lead to new bubbles appearing. Next, remove the blisters from the coating by scraping them with a brush or spatula, then sand it to obtain a uniform surface. If necessary, apply a fine filler to smooth the surface to be repainted, making sure to remove the dust after the smoothing filler has completely dried.

Next, proceed to the application of a suitable undercoat, followed by the application of finishing coats of paint. For satin or gloss paints and strong colours, it is recommended to repaint the entire surface to avoid streaks.

If bubbles persist despite these precautions, it is crucial to understand the cause of the problem, such as excessive moisture in the substrate or incorrect application of the paint. Also, be sure to maintain an appropriate room temperature for applying the paint and avoid mixing incompatible products to prevent new bubbles from appearing.

How to paint without blistering?

To prevent bubbles and blisters from forming when painting, here are some precautions to take when preparing the surface to be painted and during application:

- Make sure the surface is completely dry before starting painting work. Wipe with a cloth if necessary .
- Make sure the paint type adheres properly to the substrate to avoid subsequent blistering.
- Prepare the surface by applying a primer undercoat to promote adhesion of the new paint, especially if the surface is porous or friable.
- Control the temperature of the room you are painting in to prevent the paint from drying too quickly or too slowly, which can cause blistering.
- Use rollers that are suitable for the paint you are using for even application and to avoid bubbles.
- Use paint that is no more than a year old to ensure freshness

and adhesion.
- Follow the recommended drying times between coats of paint to avoid blistering and bubbling problems.
- Avoid rolling the roller too quickly during application to reduce the risk of bubbles forming.

Bubbles and blisters in paint can often be avoided by following these preventative steps. By carefully following these tips and taking the necessary precautions, you can achieve a smooth, flawless paint finish for your renovation project.

How to renovate an old or damaged staircase?

You want to arrange a concrete staircase by covering the steps with wood, to make it more aesthetic and warm. Here is the solution.

SUMMARY

- What budget for covering a staircase?
- What are the assembly steps?
- Special parts

The inevitable wear and tear of a staircase over the years may require renovation to transform it into a real decorative element in your interior.

What budget for covering a staircase?

The budget varies depending on the type of wood used, the price of oak or beech not being the same as that of an OSB board (pressed and glued pieces of wood). Obviously, this choice can be imposed by the location of the staircase in the house . If it is in the entrance or in the middle of the living room, it makes sense to turn to noble woods. We opted for plywood, resistant and quite affordable.

Low price

This kit, sold for €129, consists of 13 rounded galvanized steel rails and 2 other pointed ones, 15 screws with wing nuts, a flexible chain element, 6 spacers for expansion joints and 2 material addition shims.

- wolfcraft.com/en

What are the assembly steps?

The assembly of the jig is really very simple, the concept being particularly well thought out. It takes a little time to understand how it works when taking the measurements, but there is nothing too complicated. Its use does not require significant DIY knowledge .[1] However, you must be focused and rigorous at all times during the process, to obtain a truly perfect result.

1. Assemble the elements

It's a bit like a big Meccano set! Assembling the different parts (rails, spacers for expansion joints , shims, etc., see box opposite) is really not complicated. They are fixed together using wing bolts, you will have no trouble handling them. The "hardest " part is ultimately choosing the elements, to find those that are best suited to the shape of the step.

---

1. http://www.lefigaro.fr/maison/dossier/bricolage-a-la-maison-tous-nos-conseils-et-idees

2. Model the template

The idea is therefore to reproduce the perimeter of the step, by creating a template. It is not easy to have the compass in your eye, to find the pieces of the right length the first time, especially in the most crooked parts of the staircase. Arm yourself with patience on your first attempts, the assembly logic comes quite quickly. Do not forget to place 2 or 3 spacers on the rail of the step nose, it is easier to transfer the shape to the board. Add a rail across the shape and tighten all the nuts well to stiffen the structure and prevent it from deforming when handling it.

3. Report the route

Before moving the template, prepare your workspace: secure the board to the workbench so that it is stable and keep the tools needed for the next steps nearby (pencil, jigsaw, etc.). Carefully lift the template out of the step. Then place it on the board, taking care to press the spacers against one side. Trace the shape using a pencil.

4. Proceed to cutting

Fit a "fine-cut" blade, suitable for cutting plywood, to your jigsaw . Follow the pencil line, moving slowly to avoid gaps. Then run a sandpaper over the edges to remove splinters and smooth out small imperfections.

To ensure good support, the surface of the step must be clean and perfectly flat. The ideal is to sand it , [2]vacuum the dust well and wipe it with a sponge . Use a special glue to fix wood to concrete .[3] Let it dry.

Special parts

---

2. http://www.lefigaro.fr/maison/poncer-un-meuble-en-bois-comment-s-y-prendre-20240109

3. http://www.lefigaro.fr/maison/qu-est-ce-que-le-beton-cellulaire-20240402

The flexible chain element	**It is designed to fit rounded shapes, such as the central column of spiral staircases.**
The sharp rails	They allow you to reach narrow areas that conventional rails cannot reach.
Adapters for adding material	They attach to the outer rail to take into account the length of the step overhang.
Spacers for expansion joints	With humidity , heat and cold, wood can swell or shrink. It is therefore important to provide space so as not to hinder the effects of expansion.

6 tips for reinforcing or securing your front door

The front door of a house is particularly a vulnerable point of access to burglaries. However, some simple measures will be enough to secure it. Discover our six tips to deter intruders.

SUMMARY

- Installing a multi-point lock
- Adding a lock
- Installation of anti-pinch corners
- Using a lock cover
- Equip yourself with a vent
- Opt for an intercom or a videophone

Unfortunately, not everyone can afford to buy an armoured door. Since the front door is often the first option for burglars, choosing effective and affordable alternatives to secure and/or reinforce it is essential. The following tips will be even more useful if you live in a risk area . It is of course possible to combine them for greater security.

Installing a multi-point lock

This lock is distinguished by the presence of 3 to 9 closing points (or bolts) positioned on the edge of the door . The entire mechanism is controlled by a simple key.

The multi-point lock **secures your front door** , because during a break-in, the force exerted by the burglars will be distributed over several points, which will make opening much more difficult.

Adding a lock

Simple but effective, the lock is a security device that has been used for centuries to **protect doors** and windows . There are different models, the most common of which are:

- **the button lock**
- **the cylinder lock**
- **the knob and cylinder lock**
- **the code lock**

The lock has the advantage of being inexpensive. In addition, its installation does not require any special skills, so DIY enthusiasts can easily handle it.

Installation of anti-pinch corners

This equipment is a metal part installed on the outline of the front door . By filling the space between the frame and the door, the anti-pinch angle prevents the introduction of a pivot bar, a tool frequently used by thieves to leverage and force the door.

Installing this equipment requires fairly advanced DIY skills .

Using a lock cover

You can also **secure your front** door by installing a lock cover. This device, also called a rosette or cylinder protector, is a part that is placed around the cylinder of the lock. We recommend that you opt for a **magnetic or combination lock cover** which have the particularity of completely hiding the barrel. Locking and unlocking are carried out using a card or a code depending on the model.

Equip yourself with a vent

It is a small metal or plastic item installed on the door frame. It allows you to open the door enough to see the visitor, without giving them the opportunity to enter your home. It allows you to open the door enough to see the visitor, without giving them the opportunity to enter your home.

Opt for an intercom or a videophone

Investing in an intercom or videophone is also a great way to improve the security of your front door. They both allow you to establish contact without opening the door. With an intercom, you can communicate with the visitor verbally, while a videophone gives you the ability to see them. It will then be up to you to decide whether or not to open your door.

How to install a plasterboard partition?

Installing a plasterboard partition, also known as placo, is a common task in construction and renovation. How to install a plasterboard partition on a metal frame?

SUMMARY

- Materials and tools
- Assemble the metal frame
- Lay the plasterboard on the frame
- Pass the electrical conduits
- Laying glass wool for insulation

- **Lay the last plasterboards**
- **Finish with adhesive mortar for plates**

Do you want to delimit interior spaces , create new rooms or separate existing areas? Why not opt for creating a plasterboard or plasterboard partition on a metal frame, easy to install and with an affordable cost.

Materials and tools

Building a plasterboard partition on a metal frame is a DIY project that is completely accessible to beginners.

Materials for building a placo partition

To build a partition , select the right materials:

- Rails and metal frame uprights
- Peripheral ground strip
- Knock-in pegs
- Insulating
- Plasterboard (e.g.: Standard grey BA13 Placoplatre, water-repellent green Placomarine, blue Phonic placo, Habito for heavy loads, etc.)
- Plasterboard screws or dowels
- Plasterboard joint coating
- Acrylic sealant cartridge

Good to know

Regardless of the plasterboard chosen, the assembly of the partition is identical.

Useful tools

To assemble your partition, you may also need:

- Meter, Ruler, Level, Square
- Pencil, Cutter
- Shears, Saw
- Grated
- Screwdriver
- Hammer
- Concrete drill bit
- Puncher

Once you have gathered these tools, you can start assembling your partition. Don't forget to equip yourself with a dust mask and protective gloves , and to get help throughout the operation.

Assemble the metal frame

The first step in installing a plasterboard partition is to install the metal frame.

Mark and trace the position of the partition on the floor , taking into account the location of the door, then trace any returns using a mason's square. Transfer these marks to the wall and ceiling with a level leaning against a long ruler, a plumb line or a laser level.

Glue a resilient strip to the floor before fixing the rails. Use screws or dowels suitable for the support, or a gun for a concrete slab. Drill approximately every 60 cm and more than 5 centimetres from the edge of the slab, in accordance with the standards of DTU 25.41.

Then measure the height from the floor to the ceiling, then subtract 1.5 centimeters to get the length of the stud. Cut the vertical studs to the correct size. Fit the stud into the bottom rail. Apply it well against the wall flush with the outline before fixing it. Place the ceiling rails above the studs and screw them in.

Embed the studs into the rails every 60 cm and check their plumbness with a spirit level. Use a crimping plier to secure them to the rails.

Lay the plasterboard on the frame

Remember to store the plasterboard in the room where the partition will be installed for several days before the start of the work[1] , in order to avoid any thermal or hygrometric shock that could damage them. On the day, cut the boards to the right size and install them by screwing them onto the uprights. Make sure to leave a space of about 1 cm between them and the floor to prevent rising damp.

Please note

If the partition has a door, cut out the uprights and fix them on either side of the door frame.

Pass the electrical conduits

Here are the different steps for running electrical conduits through a partition:

For electrical circuits:

Run the electrical conduits to their distribution point using the holes provided for this purpose on the frame uprights.

To recess electrical boxes:

Use recessed boxes specifically designed for drywall.

---

1. http://www.lefigaro.fr/maison/dossier/maison-quelles-autorisations-pour-quels-travaux

For installing sockets and switches:

A hole saw is usually sufficient. Mark the drilling point, make a circular cut with the hole saw, then insert the box through the hole and secure it with screws.

For a junction box:

Trace the shape onto the plate, drill at the four corners, then use a small drywall saw to make the necessary straight cuts.

If electrical work seems complicated to you, call in a professional electrician who will handle this part for you.

Laying glass wool for insulation

A standard plasterboard does not provide any particular thermal or acoustic insulation . To improve these performances, you can add insulation in the thickness of the partition, such as:

- **Glass wool**
- **Rock wool**
- **Hemp wool**
- **From PSE**
- **XPS (extruded polystyrene)**
- **Or wood fiber**

Depending on your specific needs, the thickness of the insulation can vary. Usually, for BA13 partitions, a glass wool thickness of 48 mm is used.

Lay the last plasterboards

Once the insulation is in place, install the plasterboard on the second side of the partition. To reinforce the rigidity of the structure, be sure to offset the vertical joint in relation to that of the first side. Also be sure to install an acrylic joint around the edge of the structure to ensure optimal sealing.

Finish with adhesive mortar for plates

Once the plates are in place, move on to the finishing touches:

Fill the gap with acrylic putty at the bottom of the boards to ensure a uniform horizontal bond.

Do the same operation at the top of the partition, at the edge of the ceiling.

Cover all screw heads with filler .[2] A second application may be necessary the next day, as the filler tends to shrink slightly. Let dry and sand with 120 grit sandpaper. Dust off .

Finish with mortar to ensure a perfect finish to your placo partition.

If you want to paint, wallpaper or tile your partition, remember to apply primer so that the surface is uniform and the future covering adheres perfectly.

Installing a plasterboard partition is not complicated, but it does require attention to detail and careful follow-through on each step. A plasterer or a professional contractor can help you.

---

2.   http://www.lefigaro.fr/maison/enduit-pour-le-mur-5-criteres-a-surveiller-20221006

7 tips for fixing to the wall without making a hole

Are you looking for solutions to hang decorative or practical items on your walls without having to drill? Whether you are a tenant, not very good at DIY or concerned about preserving the integrity of your walls, there are ingenious alternatives to avoid holes. Discover our tips.

SUMMARY

- Double-sided adhesive
- Fixing paste
- The super strong glue
- Adhesive tabs
- Adhesive hooks

- **Magnetic paint**
- **Adhesive screws**

Wall mounting does not necessarily mean drilling, holes or major DIY work. It is indeed entirely possible to securely mount your objects without damaging your walls . Here are our alternatives.

Double-sided adhesive

Using double-sided tape can be a handy way to attach items to walls without having to drill holes . Available from hardware stores , double-sided tape comes in rolls or strong adhesive strips that can hold up to five kilos. There are also specialist adhesive strips for outdoor use, ideal for attaching mailboxes or birdhouses .

It is easy to use and install. Simply cut the adhesive strip to the desired size, apply it to the object to be fixed, and then stick it to the wall. In just a few moments, a picture, shelf or mirror is securely fixed without the need for drilling.

Double-sided adhesive can be used on different types of smooth surfaces such as:

- **The plaster**
- **The wood**
- **PVC**
- **The metal**
- **Or the glass**

Once applied, it is invisible, which guarantees an aesthetic result. It can also be used in humid rooms.

Fixing paste

Fixing paste (commonly called fixing paste) offers an ingenious solution for fixing objects to the wall without having to make a hole. There are two types:

1) **The fixing paste in the form of modeling clay** is particularly suitable for hanging frames , paintings or kitchen utensils . Simply apply an appropriate amount of paste to the object to be fixed, then press it against the wall. This paste adheres effectively to many supports such as concrete ,[1] cement or tiles , and can support a maximum load ranging from 2 to 6 kg depending on the model.

2) **The fixing paste in the form of pre-cut pads** is reusable and ideal for sticking photos or posters, with a load capacity of up to 250 g.

Easy to apply and reuse, it hardens quickly after application, ensuring a strong and reliable adhesion. In addition, it leaves no trace on walls or wall tiles, thus preserving their integrity when the paste is removed. However, avoid using it on more fragile wallpaper .

The super strong glue

Super strong glue holds objects light or heavy, both indoors and outdoors. Designed to adhere to a variety of substrates and materials, this mastic glue eliminates the need to drill or brace objects.

Its use is simple: apply beads of extra strong glue to the back of the object, then press it against the wall for a few seconds. Complete drying is done in 24 hours. Sold in cartridges to be placed in an extruder gun, the extra strong glue can fix up to 350 kg/m2, depending on the model.

You can attach XXL frames, shelves that can hold several kilos, or even a mailbox to the facade of your house . Resistant to frost, humidity and vibrations, it is also suitable for outdoor use. Suitable for a variety

---

1.   http://www.lefigaro.fr/maison/comment-entretenir-et-proteger-le-beton-cire-20220831

of substrates such as stone ,[2] brick ,[3] wood, tiles or plaster, the super powerful glue provides a strong and long-lasting bond.

Adhesive tabs

The adhesive strips can hold up to 5 kilos and are ideal for a variety of surfaces, such as painted walls, tiles, stainless steel , plastic or glass.

These adhesive tabs work in pairs: one is attached to the wall and the other to the object to be hung, the two adhering to each other thanks to a system of spikes. Their generous length allows you to keep your decorative object securely in place.

In addition, they are easily removed without leaving any trace, thus offering maximum flexibility and practicality in decorating your interior. With the adhesive tabs, you can hang your frames and photos wherever you want, without compromising the integrity of your walls and without the hassle of drilling.

Adhesive hooks

Adhesive hooks can be placed anywhere and are perfect for hanging small items such as keys, kitchen utensils, tea towels or even clothes . There are two main types of adhesive hooks: suction cup hooks and those with an adhesive mounting system.

- **Suction cup hooks** can be moved around as you wish, and are particularly suitable for smooth, damp surfaces such as shower tiles .[4] Some models can hold up to 3 kg, with enough hanging capacity for a variety of objects.

---

2.   http://www.lefigaro.fr/jardin/comment-entretenir-une-terrasse-en-pierre-20220427

3.   http://www.lefigaro.fr/maison/parement-brique-bois-comment-choisir-son-revetement-mural-20220919

4. http://www.lefigaro.fr/maison/douche-ou-baignoire-que-choisir-pour-votre-salle-de-bains-20240130

- **Adhesive hooks** can hold up to two kilos and are particularly suitable for kitchens and bathrooms . Some models combine a suction cup and a pressure system for a more secure attachment, reducing the risk of falling.

Magnetic paint

Magnetic paint is an innovative and creative solution to transform any part of your wall into a functional magnetic board. Loaded with ferrous particles, it allows you to easily hang photos, posters, memos and other items using magnets.

Available in a variety of colors, magnetic paint is easy to apply, provided the surface is carefully prepared. It can even be covered with wallpaper or thin veneer while retaining its magnetic properties. However, due to its relatively high cost, it is generally reserved for small wall surfaces.

Adhesive screws

Adhesive screws are used to attach objects to rough surfaces such as brick or stone, but they are also suitable for wood, plastic, metal, and more. Their versatility makes them suitable for both indoor and outdoor use.

Available in different shapes (round, rectangular or triangular), they simply stick to the wall. Then wait 12 hours, then fix the desired object by tightening the nut provided. Depending on the model, these screws can support a weight ranging from 2.5 to 7 kg.

An additional advantage is their ease of removal: to remove the adhesive screw, you simply turn it slowly using pliers ,[5] which helps preserve the surface on which it was attached.

To avoid drilling into your walls, these seven tips are excellent alternatives for easily fixing decorations or wall elements. Very effective,

---

5.   http://www.lefigaro.fr/maison/les-indispensables-de-la-caisse-a-outils-20240201

the strongest ones can even support up to several kilos without failing. All that's left to do is make your choice.

What to do in case of a radiator leak?

Whether it is a cast iron, steel or aluminum radiator, a radiator leak can occur for various reasons. What are the reasons why your radiator can leak? What are the consequences of this breakdown and the steps to follow to repair the leak yourself? Our answers.

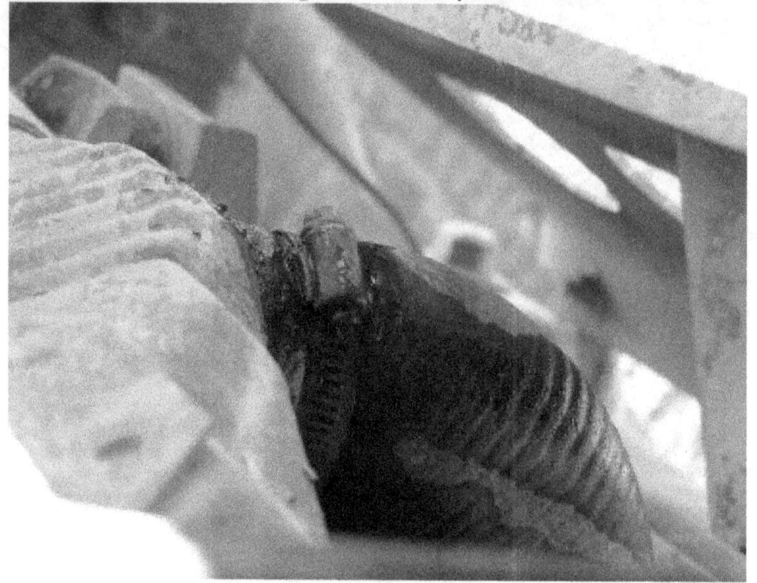

SUMMARY

- Why is my radiator leaking?
- What to do in case of a radiator leak?
- How to Fix a Radiator Leak Yourself?

Quickly identifying the causes of a radiator leak is important to prevent any potential damage to your home and your boiler .

Why is my radiator leaking?

Leaking radiators can be an annoying and potentially damaging problem for your central heating system . Here are the main reasons why your radiator might be leaking:

- **Seal wear** is common over time. The seals then lose their seal, causing leaks .[1] Check the condition of the seals occasionally and replace them if necessary.
- **A faulty supply hose** can also be the cause of a leak. Repair hose leaks quickly to prevent further damage.
- **Poorly performed bleeding** can cause leaks. Do not hesitate to call a professional to bleed your central heating circuit.
- **Faucets and valves can leak** due to wear or corrosion. Inspect them regularly.
- **Air build-up in the** heating system can cause leaks. Bleed radiators at least twice a year to remove air.
- **Lack of regular maintenance** can contribute to leaks by allowing residue or sludge to build up.

What to do in case of a radiator leak?

When you notice a leak in your heating radiator, act quickly to avoid wasting water and protect the efficiency of your heating system. Here are the steps to follow in the event of a radiator leak:

1) Immediately turn off the power to your central heating and shut off the main water supply to limit the damage and prevent any further leaks.

2) Keep calm: Although the leak may impact the operation of the radiator, it does not necessarily mean that a complete replacement is

---

1. http://www.lefigaro.fr/maison/loi-warsmann-puis-je-etre-rembourse-apres-une-fuite-d-eau-20231026

necessary. In many cases, simple repairs can be carried out, either by yourself or by calling a plumbing professional .

If the leak is coming from the radiator valve, you can often fix the problem yourself by following a few simple steps. For example, a leak caused by worn seals, faulty fittings or a loose nut can be repaired without the need for professional assistance. However, if you are unsure about the cause of the leak or are unsure about the cause of the leak, it is best to contact a qualified heating engineer to ensure an effective and safe repair.

How to Fix a Radiator Leak Yourself ?

If you are faced with a radiator leak (water radiator, gas heated) and you want to undertake the repairs yourself, here are the steps to follow:

- Immediately turn off the water supply and central heating to limit potential damage, as seen previously.
- Bleed the heating system by opening the radiator bleed screw and collecting the water that flows into a container. Close the screw when clean water begins to flow.
- Restore pressure to the heating circuit and check the condition of the gaskets and nuts, tightening them if necessary.
- Replace worn or damaged gaskets and consider flushing the radiator if necessary.
- If there is a persistent leak in the supply pipe, make a temporary repair with silicone or specialist sealant.

If the leak persists despite your efforts, call a qualified professional to diagnose and repair the problem effectively before you have unpleasant surprises with your bill.

In short, when faced with a radiator leak, it is more than advisable to act quickly. If you do not feel comfortable carrying out the repairs yourself or if you are afraid of making the situation worse, call a professional at the first sign of a problem. Radiator leaks can cause considerable damage, not only to your heating system and your home, but also financially. Do not delay in reacting to avoid later complications.

Cracked sink: how to repair it easily?

All it takes is a clumsy move for a heavy object to crack your kitchen sink or bathroom sink. Fortunately, with a sealant and a little skill, your bathroom will be almost as good as new.

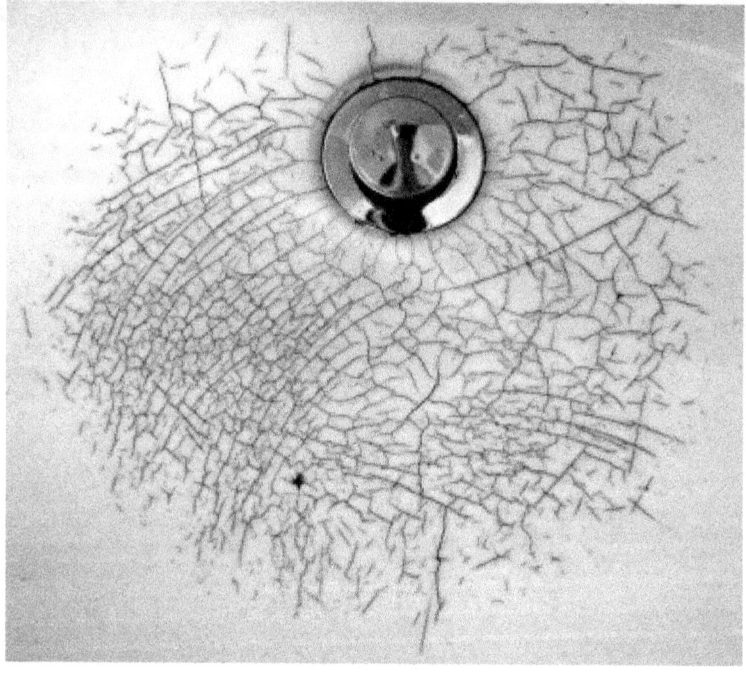

SUMMARY

- 1. Preparations before repair
- Cleaning and degreasing the sink
- Sanding the cracked sink and preparing the resin mix
- Application of the sealing product
- Application of protective paint

It is not always necessary to replace a damaged sink . If the crack is not too big, a repair is often possible. By carrying out this DIY operation accessible to all yourself, you will significantly extend the life of your sanitary ware for only a few euros. Our advice for **repairing a cracked sink** in 5 steps.

1. Preparations before repair

The necessary material :

- a spatula;
- a sponge ;
- a rag;
- an adjustable wrench ;
- a set of screwdrivers;
- a pair of pliers;
- a small foam paint roller;
- fine sandpaper;
- white vinegar;
- a two-component epoxy resin kit;
- Epoxy paint for sanitary facilities;
- latex or nitrile gloves;
- protective glasses;
- a breathing mask.

Dismantling the cracked sink

This step is not mandatory. But to facilitate access to the area to be repaired or to work more comfortably, it is sometimes preferable to disassemble the cracked sink.

Cleaning and degreasing the sink

Thorough cleaning using a standard household product allows **the sealant to adhere** to the sanitary ware. For degreasing, we recommend using white vinegar, a natural product whose effectiveness is well known. Once cleaning is complete, rinse and wipe the sink with a dry cloth.

Sanding the cracked sink and preparing the resin mix

Sanding the cracked sink creates a rough surface, which makes it easier for the sealant to adhere. Sand the surface to be treated using your sandpaper. Then clean your sanitary ware again to remove any sanding residue.

Epoxy resin is usually made up of two components: **a resin and a hardener** . Follow the manufacturer's instructions for mixing. Be sure to wear gloves, goggles and a mask, as this product is extremely toxic.

Application of the sealing product

Using a spatula, apply **the epoxy resin** to the crack . Then let it dry for the time recommended in the instructions for use.

Once the resin is completely dry, you can proceed to sand the repaired area. This will give you a smooth and uniform surface. Keep your protective equipment on, as sanding residue is also very harmful.

Application of protective paint

It is possible that the color of your paint is not exactly the same as that of your sink. If this is the case, it will be necessary to apply paint to the entire surface of the sanitary ware. You will therefore have to sand it completely so that it adheres properly.

After cleaning the sink, you will only have to apply a coat of **Epoxy paint** to obtain an impeccable finish.

Power failure: how to find and resolve it?

Blocked roller shutters, unusable oven, garage door that remains open... Electrical faults can disrupt our daily lives. How to find the origin of an electrical fault? And how to resolve it? Answers from an electrician.

SUMMARY

- How to find the cause of an electrical fault?
- Power outage: where to start?
- Faulty sockets and switches: how to identify them?
- Power strips and extension cords: sources of problems
- A faulty device: what electrical problem?
- What are the most common electrical failures?
- Electricity: Things not to do

Suddenly, the house is plunged into darkness. When you come home from work, the ceiling light no longer works. The house alarm rings continuously. Could it be an electrical problem? Finding and fixing an electrical fault may seem complex at first, but with the advice of an electrician, here's how to do it.

How to find the cause of an electrical fault?

Before getting started, Patrick Magisson, manager of an electrical company in Oise, stresses the importance of knowing the electrical installation of your home . *"Where is the electrical panel? Are there several? Are they complete and all connected to a specific area of the house?"*

With a good knowledge of your installation, you can carry out in-depth tests to identify the source of the breakdown. However, if this is not the case, take the time to find out about the safety standards and the electrical installation of your home . If in doubt, it is imperative to call a professional to avoid any risk.

The first step in finding an electrical fault is to identify the source of the problem. To do this, you need to look at your **electrical panel** . According to Patrick Magisson, *"many individuals frequently confuse the meter and the electrical panel. The meter is the element that measures the amount of energy consumed in a place, thus allowing electricity suppliers to calculate the consumption of the home. It is installed in the electrical panel, which brings together all the controls for the low-voltage electrical installation in your home. On the other hand, the circuit breakers and fuses, also present in the electrical panel, are designed to protect the electrical installation in your home. "*

Good to know

Don't forget to take a look outside to see if the outage is also affecting your neighbors . If so, contact your electricity supplier first.

Power outage: where to start?

To find a fault, you must therefore check whether one of the circuit breakers in your electrical panel is in the "OFF" (or 0) position. If this is the case, you must try to put it back in the "ON" (or 1) position. If the circuit breaker trips again immediately, this may indicate a voltage problem. You must therefore investigate and find the reason for this outage.

If all your circuit breakers are in the "ON" position, it is essential to check the fuses to determine if they are damaged. To do this safely, turn off the main power. Once the power is off, use insulated pliers to remove each fuse. This careful inspection of the network will allow you to spot any visible signs of faults, such as damaged cables or burnt fuses (is the indicator lamp intact? Has the filament burned out?).

If your fuse is defective, it must be replaced. Be sure to choose a fuse model with the same amperage as indicated on the fuse holder.

Faulty sockets and switches : how to identify them?

Most electrical outages are caused by faulty electrical outlets or switches . When your circuit breaker won't stay in the "ON" position in a specific area of your home, it's necessary to conduct a thorough investigation to identify the source of the fault.

"It is essential to ensure that the sockets are correctly inserted into the wall and that the pins of electrical devices are inserted correctly ," explains Patrick Magisson.

He then suggests a simple method to check the functioning of the sockets: " *You can plug in a device such as a bedside lamp . If the lamp lights up and your installation does not trip, move to another socket. If, during the test, the lamp did not light up and the circuit breaker 'tripped', then the problem is indeed linked to your electrical installation: either the socket is faulty, or the electrical circuit that goes from the circuit breaker to the socket is damaged."*

In such situations, disassembling the outlet to examine for potential problems is an essential step. The wires may simply be loose, in which case simply reattach them to make good contact, then tighten them with a small screwdriver. However, it may also happen that they are split, or that the presence of water or pests such as mice has damaged them. It is then recommended to call an electrician to ensure that other outlets do not have the same problems.

Finally, it is important to test each switch by operating it to verify that it is working properly. If one of them fails to turn the light on or off, it could be faulty or poorly connected.

To do this, remove the cover plate that covers the switch using a flathead screwdriver, then unscrew the switch from its flush-mounting box. Check that the wires are not cut, make sure that they are properly connected and correctly inserted into their terminals, and tighten the cable fasteners if necessary.

Attention

Before any manipulation, it is imperative to turn off your electrical circuit by cutting the power supply via the main circuit breaker. Check that there is no voltage at its output. This precaution is crucial to avoid any risk of electric shock during your interventions.

Power strips and extension cords: sources of problems

Power strips and extension cords can cause a lot of problems. According to our electrician, it is *"strongly discouraged, if not forbidden, to use extension cords and then connect power strips to them, because this generally causes "electrical heating" on the unwinder or on the extension cord, thus causing a power cut."*

In the event of a power outage, remove all power strips to directly access the power supply at the wall outlet. Perform the lamp test again to identify the source of your power outage. Finally, any signs of sparks, burns, or a burning smell could indicate a problem with either the outlet itself or the device plugged into it.

A faulty device: what electrical problem?

A faulty appliance can cause various problems in your electrical system including:

- a short circuit: in this case, the circuit breaker concerned trips to interrupt the power supply and prevent any incident
- a current leak, if for example a bare wire touches the metal casing of the appliance: in this case, the differential switch trips and cuts off the electrical installation to ensure the safety of the occupants of the house

It is therefore essential to quickly identify the faulty device. In general, this device stops working or presents episodic and abnormal malfunctions.

However, if you can't identify it, simply unplug the devices, reset the lowered circuit breaker, and then plug the instruments back in one by one. If a device is the cause of the power failure, the power should trip again when you reconnect it. It is then advisable to replace the faulty device or take it to a professional repairer. If it is your alarm, intercom , electric garage , contact an electrician.

Please note that some electrical devices are equipped with capacitors, which can deliver a high electrical voltage several seconds after the power is cut off. The slightest internal manipulation of the device can put you in danger. It is therefore advisable to contact a professional repairer.

What are the most common electrical failures?

- **Power outages:** general power outage, linked to the electricity supplier
- **Outdated electrical installation:** it no longer meets safety standards and is subject to variations.
- **Electrical equipment faults:** power strip, kettle, toaster, radiator , etc.
- **Insulation fault:** poor insulation on a device or a poorly made connection can cause a current leak.
- **Faulty electrical outlet:** If one of your electrical outlets is worn or improperly installed, the circuit breaker may trip the power.
- **Water phenomenon in the devices:** this can cause malfunctions and cuts.

Electricity: Things not to do

In your daily life or in your electrical repairs, it is possible that you make imprudent gestures. In order to prevent any accident, here are some rules of caution:

- Never use a damaged extension cord.
- Never use a faulty electrical appliance.
- Before changing a lamp bulb, unplug it or turn off the power using the switch.
- Make sure to locate electrical wires before drilling into a wall .
- In the bathroom , never use electrical appliances if you are wet or if the humidity is high.
- Do not use electrical appliances or extension cords near a swimming pool .
- If a circuit breaker in your distribution panel trips frequently,

distribute your appliances to other circuits.

- Do not cut or bend the third prong of a plug.
- Never throw water on a burning electrical outlet .
- Be careful when removing the cover plate from a switch or electrical outlet.

Pro tip

"Before undertaking electrical work, it is crucial to find out about current standards and determine whether the individual is capable of carrying out a correct and safe installation. If in doubt or if the problem persists, consult a professional to ensure the safety of your installation." Patrick Magisson, electrician.

Don't miss out!

Visit the website below and you can sign up to receive emails whenever RC PRABIR publishes a new book. There's no charge and no obligation.

https://books2read.com/r/B-A-AAWFB-JULIF

BOOKS 2 READ

Connecting independent readers to independent writers.

Did you love *DIY House Hacks: Clever Fixes for Modern Living*? Then you should read *When Nightmares Breathe : Unearthly Stories That Grip the Soul*[1] by Prabir Rai Chaudhuri!

[2]

When Nightmares Breathe: Unearthly Stories That Grip the Soul

In the quiet of the night, when shadows stretch and darkness closes in, our deepest fears come alive. "When Nightmares Breathe" invites you into a world where the line between reality and the supernatural blurs, where the unknown whispers your name, and where every flicker of light could be the last you see.

Within these pages, you'll encounter tales that will make your heart race and your spine tingle. From the chilling echo of footsteps in an empty corridor to the haunting stare of eyes that aren't there, each story delves into the darkest corners of the human psyche. These are

---

1. https://books2read.com/u/3n1N75

2. https://books2read.com/u/3n1N75

the stories that slip into your thoughts long after you've turned the last page, lingering in the periphery of your mind like a shadow you can't shake.

This collection doesn't just tell stories—it ensnares you, pulling you into a world where fear is not just a feeling, but a living, breathing entity. Each narrative is carefully crafted to grip your soul, unraveling the familiar and replacing it with the unknown. As you journey through the eerie landscapes and unsettling encounters, you'll find yourself questioning the reality of your own world.

Perfect for those who crave the thrill of suspense and the chill of horror, "When Nightmares Breathe" offers a reading experience like no other. Prepare yourself—these stories aren't just read, they are felt, and they will haunt you long after the last word is written.

Also by RC PRABIR

DIY House Hacks
DIY House Hacks: Clever Fixes for Modern Living